Resistance

Voices of Exiled Writers

Palewell Press

Resistance
Voices of Exiled Writers

Exiled Writers Ink

Resistance, Exiled Writer Ink

First edition 2020 from Palewell Press, www.palewellpress.co.uk

Printed and bound in the UK

ISBN 978-1-911587-46-0

A CIP catalogue record for this title is available from the British Library.

Acknowledgements

We express our deep gratitude to all the contributing poets and writers.

Thanks are due to Amir Darwish for his help providing information and insights for the chapter on Syrian writers.

Thank you to Simone Theiss, whose work at https://ciluna27.wordpress.com/ draws attention to human rights violations around the world, for her contributions to the chapters on Iranian Women in Prison, and Words for the Silenced.

Thank you to Dr Nazand Begikhani for sharing the narrative 'The Black Hands', which was among those that emerged from a research project on 'Gender-based Violence and Displacement', led by the University of Bristol's Centre for Gender and Violence Research https://www.nazandbegikhani.com/info/university-of-bristol-gender-based-violence-and-displacement-647

Thank you to Dr Anba Jawi for bringing our attention to the works of the Iraqi protest poets, and for her translations.

Dedication

This anthology is dedicated to all those resisting oppression in all its many forms and to those who died fighting for their just cause.

Contents

Introduction

Exiled Writers Ink joyfully celebrates the 20th year of our existence with this book of Resistance. In fact, our organisation was born of resistance.

At a time when refugees were frequently stigmatised as disempowered, uneducated victims intent on exploiting the host society's welfare and other systems, Exiled Writers Ink was set on defying that narrative to disrupt existing stereotypes. With a passion for justice, we enabled refugee writers' voices to be heard so that insights could be gained, not only into the pain suffered by refugees, but also into the complexity of the experiences of writers from diverse regions.

This special book, by the Exiled Writers Ink editorial committee, comprises one chapter for each of the twenty years between 2000, when the organisation was formally established, and 2020. Each chapter represents an aspect of our literary activism work in the context of individual and collective resistance against the abuse of human rights. While we have linked our projects and activities to specific years, in so many instances the specific human rights abuse and/or conflict has a long history and endures.

Yet the main focus must be on the voices of the exiled writers themselves with those we feature having almost all been involved with Exiled Writers Ink. Their poetry and prose represent the intersection of the personal and the political. Politics is inextricably linked with the literary work of writers who fled from their countries because of oppression, persecution, war, imprisonment, lack of freedom of speech and more. To be an exiled writer is to use writing as a tool to speak out against continuing injustice and abuse in the country of origin. With this courage comes risk, even in exile.

In this book manifold forms of resistance reveal themselves. Resistance is commonly seen as the act or power of opposing a situation and is motivated above all by a desire for justice. Indeed, the call for revolution itself is heard in a couple of poems here. While the writing acts to defiantly contest iniquities such as persecution, violence, oppression, injustice and corruption, it also functions as witness to appalling deeds. As such, it insists on the imperative of remembering, warning against amnesia, memory distortion or denial often imposed by the ruling power. The writers are compelled to remember, to recall, to share the truth in order to counter political distortions of history itself. Memory manifests itself too in the refusal to allow collective history to be effaced. Nostalgia plays a role in maintaining the writer's idealised memory which generates strength and the will to engage in the struggle of the homeland. Yet, the poetics also function to challenge and unsettle deep-seated divides, be they religious, nationalistic or ethnic. Throughout, resilience prevails, in itself a refusal to be daunted.

In all its 20 years of existence, Exiled Writers Ink has stood for advocating human rights and tolerance through literature and literary activism. We stand in solidarity with the struggle for truth, humanity and justice.

Exiled Writers Ink, www.exiledwritersink.co.uk, brings together established, emerging and aspiring writers from repressive regimes and war-torn situations and equally embraces migrants. Providing a safe, welcoming space, the organisation encourages cross-cultural dialogue and advocates human rights through literature and literary activism. Over the years the network has developed creative writing workshops, mentoring and translation services, publications (including *Exiled Ink* magazine), live literature events, theatre productions, symposia and poetry competitions.

Dr Jennifer Langer, Exiled Writers Ink founder & director

The Exiled Writers Ink editorial committee:
Dr David Clark, Catherine Davidson,
Fatima Hagi, Dr Jennifer Langer, Esther Lipton,
Danielle Maisano, Dr Denise Saul

2000
Speaking Out about Kosova

Cast your mind back to Kosova in 1999. Terrible atrocities were being committed - homes torched, families uprooted, innocent people murdered, including children and pregnant women. Given the intense media coverage, we questioned why a mass protest and resistance movement had not emerged outside Kosova to prevent the escalation into horror and to help the resistance inside Kosova with arms, food and medical supplies.

Profoundly troubled by the international community's indifference and powerlessness to prevent the 'ethnic cleansing', Exiled Writers Ink held a high-profile solidarity event at which Kosovan and Bosnian writers and UK journalists gave impassioned speeches to a packed audience. Although the pain everyone felt was immense, all were determined to speak out in an act of shared witnessing and anger. In their refusal to be cowed, the Kosovans were clear that they would determine their own way forward and that they and their collective history would not be effaced. Their words resonated with the resolve of resistance: the Kosovan people would return to rebuild their homes and lives in their land and would not relinquish Kosova. In the words of Behxhet Muharremi, 'One day Kosova will be free.'

A few summers later at the first international FLO festival of literature by serene Lake Batllava in Kosova, some Exiled Writers Ink writers were engaged in creative synergy with those from south-eastern European countries. Word about our London event had reached Kosovans and we were surprised and humbled at the appreciation expressed by them.

By Jennifer Langer

By Kalvar

Each passing day
resembles the one today
I'm one of those
narrators of the
modern age
of the Golgota* in the Balkans.
Monotonously observing
the usual empty corners
noting persecutions sowing fear
And Kalvar stands dignified
outside the ancient walls of the fortress
the ancient altar of savages
gorging on the blood of askets*

By Aida Dërguti
Translated by Lindita Dërguti Pajaziti

* Golgota – evil army
* askets – a religion. The followers believe people should enjoy pain
and sacrifice in order to ensure a better life in the other world.

A Drama

NEVER fight against life
DO NOT let the horses get lost on the paths
REMEMBER the dogs barking like mad
and the sofra* laid without bread
DO NOT open the doors to the wounds
LISTEN!
THE BLOOD will flood
A WHOLE DRAMA on a small stage

By Valbona Ismaili Luta
Translated from the Albanian by Ragip Luta

* dinner table

Blues for My Dead Friends

I will get drunk
I will get as drunk as a lord
With my old friends
Mirko Mark Gashi
Will put me in his right arm
Hajdar Salihu will be in my left arm
We will drink
For the first time
In silence undisturbed by the living
We will drink so much
That I will make them forget they have died
I will lie that the freedom came
That neither do spies spy
Nor do they harass poets
So that the graves do not remain empty
I will fill them with one of my halves
Which I will steal from my dead self
If they miss me
Let them call me again
To strike out as we once did
Glasses one after another
Well, to be honest
It's quite boring without them

By Abdullah Konushevci
Translated from the Albanian by Vlora Konushevci

Peace to All People

No apology
to the unjust soldiers
no apology
to the poison holders
no apology
to the robbers of light
no apology
to those who love to fight.
No apology
to the breakers of hearts
to those who hate the sun of life.
No apology
to the lovers of wars
no apology
to the closers of life's doors.

God, don't let people die
to the enemies of freedom
                No apology

By Brikena Muharremi

2001
Violence against Women:
The Words of Women

Patriarchal control is violence against women whose anger is palpable in the poetry here. They write to expose and resist the victimisation of women by patriarchal societies in which power structures and conflict connect with the oppression of women.

In many traditionally patriarchal societies boys are educated to become men who practise control over women. Girls are brought up to be submissive, motherhood their only acceptable role. Kurdish Iraqi writer, Nazand Begikhani, writes defiantly about social control in her community in the name of religion, culture and tradition, deemed to define identity by the community. Members are compelled to observe patriarchal social norms to retain unity and continuity as otherwise they will be subject to exclusion and violence. In fact, in so many countries there is enormous pressure on women to conform. To deviate is dangerous.

The 'honour' ethos is based on the belief that women cannot be trusted to protect their chastity in the best interests of patriarchal society. A woman may be killed for exercising her autonomy: for choosing a man to marry that the family has not selected, for having a love affair, for eloping, or for joining a political party – anything might trigger a sense the woman has brought dishonour and shame to the extended family. Punitive killings can be carried out by a woman's father, husband, brother or other male relatives. The suspected murder by her father of 14-year old Romina Ashrafi in 2020, after she ran away from home with a 29-year-old man, attests to the continuing violence that can erupt at any time.

Exile is not necessarily accompanied by freedom from the traditional patriarchal structures that limited women's lives in their homelands. In *Forbidden Zones* (2013) Aydin Mehmet Ali's powerful short stories give voice to women silenced by taboos to expose diasporic patriarchal violence. Other women

too, resist patriarchal narratives through articulating the pain of
gender-based violence, turning injustice into poetry and prose.

By Jennifer Langer

My Mother Pictured Amongst Tobacco Leaves

Your picture in the greenness of the tobacco
leaves
reflecting the light of the Orient
you bend among the endless lines
of the staring tobacco plants
like doubt after conviction
you pick up the leaves
lay them in the *Charoga*
hanging at your neck
and carry them to the *Ber Heywan*
Piles of sad leaves
Piles of silence
hidden under the *Nur* of the Orient

Your wrinkled hands
talk to me
tell the story of a stolen childhood
the loneliness of women in my homeland

I look at your fingers
you place the leaves one by one on the tobacco *shish*
threading them like long beads into a necklace
then you kneel before this heap of tobacco necklaces
place them on your back,
climb the hill to reach the *Chardagh*
and hang them in precise lines
to dry

Infinite lines of tobacco necklaces
Infinite scars on your heart

I can feel your body drying up
like the tobacco plant in the midsummer heat
and your life
your life similar to the tobacco leaves
has been picked and burnt away
like a cigarette
between a man's fingers.

By Nazand Begikhani

Romina

In memory of Romina Ashrafi, a 14-year-old girl who is the latest victim of honour killing in Iran.

Romina is lying in a pool of crimson
A sickle has pierced her heart
Withered white wings of an angel, smeared
with blood, as though she has been
visited by the angel of death
The sickle glimmers in the moonlight
as thirteen years of innocent life
drain away, one by one
Thirteen doves fly away with blood stained wings…
Romina was a good student
Romina was a kind daughter
The sickle belongs to her father
The blood had to be shed to restore honour
To wipe away the shame she has bestowed upon the family
Romina's body is now purified
To be honourably prayed for and buried
Romina's tears still glistening on her pale cheeks
Romina's honour is restored.

By Shirin Razavian

The Ten-Year-Old Bride

Forced into her starry dress

It was as if they had shaken the night
                              over her
And her murky tears
Suppurating from fear's sores
In a tribe with its mummified laughter
And quadruped hoof prints
On their sludge of imagination
The ten-year-old bride
                    Ten-year-old child
They drag
               drag   drag her
to her husband's stronghold
Do you want your doll?
                         Your doll died!
Last night
Fairy tale giants
Mounted an assault
Murdered your father
Abducted your mother
Devoured your playmates
And your doll?
          Crushed underfoot

                              died!
But isn't she the ludicrous lineage of her mother?
A long wearisome chapter
An agonising likeness
                    taking refuge in her inner turmoil?
The bludgeon of inherited mores
                    on her head

The bludgeon of inherited fear and superstition
          on her head
The bludgeon of inherited silence
                    on her head
Her today is buried
                         under yesterday's debris
And maturity?
Like the throes of ancient marshes!
Where should she sleep?
                         to set her fearless dream   free
She felt
Her breath withering the flowers
"I'm asleep
                    it's a nightmare!
I'm asleep
                    it's a nightmare!
                              tomorrow…"
Tomorrow?!
Tomorrow's dawn
                         pitch black
The city turned upside down
Your father is an ogre
Your mother is a vampire
Your husband?
               He is the demon of fairy tales!
And the dust
engulfed her so that
no one could see
the wind blowing her
               away

By Mehrangiz Rassapour (M. Pegah)
Translated from the Persian by Catherine Davidson

I am Neda

On June 20th 2009, Neda Agha-Soltan, a 26 year old Iranian woman who was demonstrating in Tehran to protest against the vote-count fraud in the re-election of President Mahmoud Ahmadinejad, was shot in the heart by a Basiji hiding on the rooftop of a civilian house.

Leave the Basiji bullet in my heart,
fall to prayer in my blood,
and hush, father
—I am not dead.
More light than mass,
I flood through you,
breathe with your eyes,
stand in your shoes, on the rooftops,
in the streets, march with you
in the cities and villages of our country
shouting through you, with you.
I am Neda—thunder on your tongue.

By Sholeh Wolpé

2002
Confronting Black Storms: Afghanistan

After the 1979 occupation of Afghanistan by the Soviet Union, the *mujahadin* waged war against the Afghan communist regime. By the mid-eighties, over a quarter of the entire Afghan population had become refugees, while internal exile was also very high. From 1992 the *mujahidin* fought against each other until the Taliban took power in 1996. In 1998 the European Union suspended all new humanitarian aid to the Taliban regime in Kabul to protest at its denial of equal treatment to women. The attack on the USA on 11th September 2001 led to the Taliban regime being attacked in Afghanistan in the search for the perpetrators, in particular Osama bin Laden and Al Qa'eda. Peace in Afghanistan has remained elusive with continued violence and atrocities, a reduction in the presence of foreign troops, the rise of new insurgents, such as the IS, and the continued presence of the Taliban in certain areas. Thousands of civilians have lost their lives and nearly a million more have been internally displaced. The prospect of civil war once again seems imminent.

In the face of a country in turmoil, writers may turn to unburdening themselves on paper in a cathartic act of mourning or in a cry of despair yet their writings also act as witness to record atrocities and destruction. In this chapter we listen as some Afghan writers raise their voices against constant occupation and war. In Hasan Bamyani's portrayal of Afghanistan as a beautiful garden that has been violated, he orders the invaders to leave. Ahmad Masood Wahed speaks out to assert that it is the leaders who are responsible for the atrocities and bloodshed and calls for love, justice and respect, while Shabibi Shah similarly calls for Afghans to embrace a culture of tolerance and shared responsibility. She speaks out about the hidden face of Afghan women in war to insist on equality in education, a social state, employment, respect and the need to follow their own culture rather than the West's. However, she is deeply fearful of the future of women in her country.

By David Clark

Poem for My Country

Gunfire
What are you doing in my garden?
Get out!
It's springtime
Flower buds are opening
Nightingales and turtle doves
Are singing
They are my beloved

Get out
Get out

By Hasan Bamyani
Translated by Carole Angier

Black Storms

My caravan with colours and fragrances
was looted completely.
The spring left me like a lotus with a spot
on its heart, alone in the desert.
The black storms of autumn surrounded
   my life.
So I could not see the difference
between the spring and autumn.

By Mojawer Ahmad Zyar

Landscape of Wounds

I am the night; my soul, my gaze, my dream are the worst
wounds
While in the shadowed mirror, my lips brush against pursed
wounds.

Autumn bleeds through each season, my Libra upsets
Sagittarius
And the arrow strikes Scorpio, releasing venom from burst
wounds.

The bull, weary and mad, will shake my Earth, which his horns
cradle.
This heart, stuck, is my donkey, crippled by unnursed wounds.

I have no sky in which to place my star, it drowns in dark;
I have no country, no land to make a grave for these cursed
wounds.

Daddy leaves me dust and blood in the place of bread and
water;
My school, which grew first words, now breeds first wounds.

Passion, logic have faded, just grey shadows in the fold
Of spirits, weakly dreaming, submitting to rehearsed wounds.

My name, my faith, my memories, even my words are scarred;
From beginning to end of this journey, I have always traversed
wounds.

By Suhrab Sirat
Translated by Claire Carlotti

The Generation of War

...The world has since defended the war in Afghanistan as an ethical struggle. Some have even branded it a religious war or the war of ideologies managed by the hands of outsiders. Well they could be right, but whom really should we Afghans blame?...We were told how to hate Pashtuns, who in turn were told to hate Tajiks, who were then told to hate Hazaras. ...We fought each other but never understood why....It was all our own naivety, particularly our belief in our leaders who ...have always used Islam as a shelter or as an excuse to deceive a nation, a nation that never had a chance to see reality.

I, as an Afghan from a new generation of war, strongly believe that our leaders... are responsible for all atrocities and bloodshed. ...Today, we Afghans are still waiting for a chance to see ...this innocent nation once again start its new life under the mantle of love, justice and respect, not the yoke of guns and the sound of fire!!

By Ahmad Masood Wahed

Shabibi Shah demonstrates personal resilience and fortitude as a woman in Afghanistan. In the extract that follows from her memoir, *Where do I Belong?,* she finds herself defending her husband who is accused of writing articles opposing the regime.

Where Do I Belong?

Zafar had nobody to support him apart from me. The court room was small, cold and silent. There were about ten people in the room and it was not clear who they were. The judge was sitting in a large chair apart from the other people, one of whom stood up and began reading the case against Zafar. When he had finished, I was relieved that there were no questions for Zafar to answer. Then it was Zafar's turn to speak. He just had to read the defence which had been prepared for him by his lawyer. Zafar was shaking and moving from one foot to another in obvious distress and I began to doubt that he could even complete this simple task. He began to read but after a few sentences made no sense and began laughing loudly. Everyone could see that he was out of control.

I could not bear to see that our opportunity to clear his name was slipping away. I stood up and asked if anyone had any objection to me reading it for him. The judge gave it some thought and asked if those present would agree to my request. Fortunately everyone did, so I took the paper from Zafar's hand and told him to sit down. It was an unusual situation as I was the only woman in court and may have been the first woman to represent her husband. In spite of the coldness, I was covered in sweat, and somehow managed to make the sounds come out of my mouth as my heartbeat faster and faster.

Slowly I began to read the paper which I had not set eyes on before. I could feel my voice echoing in the deadly silence of the court room, and I knew that all eyes were on my burning face. I do not remember what I read, but I know that the legal wording was unfamiliar. Zafar was sitting next to me and would occasionally stand up and sit down again which was very distracting. I was sure that nothing I read was registering in his troubled mind. He was playing with his fingers like a child.

When I had finished I was exhausted and felt quite faint, needing a glass of water and some fresh air. We were given a fifteen-minute break and then we went back into the court room. As I took my place next to Zafar, someone whispered, "You are a brave woman and I admire your courage in helping your husband." I thanked him but thought how much I would prefer to live a quiet life like an ordinary woman. We waited for a long time and then the judge declared Zafar innocent. I could not believe what I was hearing. In my heart I felt such gratitude to the Minister of the Interior. Zafar was innocent but it had taken me eight long months to prove it.

By Shabibi Shah

In the Name of Kabul

My presence is here but
My heart reposes in the alleyways of Kabul.
My tongue utters its name
My lips sing an anthem of Kabul.
Trees shrouded in inky-blue
Years, months, weeks, days, mourning Kabul.
Oh traveller! Traverse my town silently
For in mourning is Kabul.
He who knows its streets, its palaces
Murmurs "Where am I?" Kabul.
Oh God, you who are both benevolent and wrathful,
Your munificence is disposed elsewhere, your anger vented on Kabul.
Mother of Rostam undeserving of this cruelty
Undeserving of this affliction, Kabul.
The hand of God must surely intervene
The hand of Satan powerless to assuage the agony of Kabul.
At dawn, the water seller bears his parched goatskin
He dreams of water, the water-seller of Kabul.
The yellow trees of the tall and gracious poplar
Rise up - a hand praying for Kabul.
As tyrants Yazed and his followers spill the blood of innocents
Oh Hassan, oh Hassan, is this the Karbala of Kabul?
The Taliban surged forth, broke down the gateways of knowledge,
    the windows of learning
Those who are illiterate, now become the spiritual teacher of Kabul.
We are plunged into the abyss of the Stone Age,
The painters of vanity now come forth as leaders of Kabul.
From annihilation, liberate Kabul, may its citizens survive.
If I live out my days, so too surely will Kabul.
If God one day pours forth his wrath on this Earth, spills blood
That would be the retribution for Kabul.

By Berang Kohdamani
Translated from Dari by Suhaila Ismat
and Jennifer Langer

2003
Forbidden: Censorship

The literary work of numerous writers involved in Exiled Writers Ink is banned in their countries of origin yet their voices of resistance against their countries' regimes continue to be heard in exile. These writers include Ziba Karbassi, Ghazi Rabihavi, Esmail Khoi and Ali Abdolrezaei from Iran, Chinese poet Yang Lian and Tibetan poet Tenzin Tsundue.

Tsundue is an activist and poet who was forcibly exiled to India from Tibet by China and has been involved in Tibet's independence movement since his student days. He caught international media attention in 2002 and 2005 when he displayed banners proclaiming 'Free Tibet: China Get Out' with the Tibetan flag when Chinese premiers were visiting India. Yet, despair can set in over the world's apathy, a sensibility conveyed in some of Tsundue's poetry. Some of his translated poems, published in Chinese by a Taiwan organisation, have been secretly disseminated in China while translations in Tibetan have been clandestinely distributed in Tibet among young and intellectual circles.

China exercises control over all Yang Lian's publications both in print and online. His work was banned in 1989 when he organised memorial services for the dead of Tiananmen while in New Zealand. Exiled from China from 1989, his books were banned for many years by the censors. In 2011 his collection *Narrative Poem* survived just one day before the copies were recalled and destroyed, the reason being that in one section Yang Lian had written about the Tiananmen Square Massacre.

Esmail Khoi has emerged as a most articulate, poetic voice in the Iranian diaspora fearlessly and courageously defending human rights and political freedom the world over. He was forced to spend almost two years in hiding in Iran because of his opposition to clerical rule, before eventually fleeing from his homeland in 1983. In 1995 he spoke out about censorship in Iran

"When I speak of censorship, I am speaking about what is happening to the whole of Iranian poetry, to the whole of Iranian literature, to the whole of Iranian art, culture and life. Yes, life itself has become the object of censorship in Iran."

Most of Ghazi Rabihavi's books remain banned in Iran including *The Boys of Love* which is the only currently published Iranian novel to deal with the theme of homosexuality there. In Iran decades of censorship, both during the Shah's reign and following the Revolution, have firmly implanted a culture of censorship within Iranian society. Writers in Iran have been arrested, imprisoned, tortured and executed. In order to obtain permission for publication in Iran, writers must submit their work to the Ministry of Culture and Islamic Guidance. Ghazi Rabihavi employs satire in his defiance of the system.

By Jennifer Langer

Once Upon a Time

Once upon a time an Iranian writer wrote a 279 page-long novel and, like every other Iranian writer, presented it to the Ministry of Islamic Guidance to receive a publication permit. The book began with the following passage:

'She knew that once her husband had brought her a cup of coffee, she would feel better, like every other day. As she stood by the window, the wind slid gently over her brown arms, and her eyes were on the rising sun that was pulling itself up over the government buildings; it was a sunrise that was like a sunset.'

After thirteen months spent climbing up the slippery ladder of bureaucracy, the Iranian writer finally managed to obtain an appointment with the director in charge of censorship. The director was just a head. His body was hidden behind the desk and it seemed to be reclining gently against something soft. The head delivered the following speech to the writer:

"Unfortunately, you book has some small problems which cannot be corrected. I am certain you will agree with me; take these first few sentences... Nowhere in our culture will you find any woman who would allow herself to stand waiting for her husband to bring her a cup of coffee. OK? Well, the next problem is the image of the wind sliding over the naked arms, which is provocative and has sexual overtones. Finally, nowhere in any noble culture will you find a sunrise that is like a sunset, maybe it is a misprint. Here you are then. Here is your book. I hope you will write another one soon. We support you." Then the head slid back under the desk.

By Ghazi Rabihavi
Translated by Nilou Mobaser

Forms of Fascism

When they shout "My Lords!"
I hear Fascism speaking.
When they shout "Brethren!"
I hear Fascism speaking.
When they should "Fellow Countrymen!"
I hear Fascism speaking.
When they shout "Comrades!"
I still hear Fascism speaking.
A World *is* to be
                in which
nobody is anybody's special somebody.

And so,
No!
Do not call me "Friend!"
Not even that, my friend!
No categorising word.
Call me by my proper name:
                Esmail.

By Esmail Khoi

I'm Tired

I am tired,
I am tired doing that 10th March ritual,
screaming from the hills of Dharamsala.
I am tired,
I am tired selling sweaters on the roadside,
40 years of sitting, waiting in dust and spit.

I am tired,
eating rice 'n' dal
and grazing cows in the jungles of Karnataka.

I am tired,
I am tired dragging my dhoti
in the dirt of Manju Tila.

I am tired,
I am tired fighting for the country
I have never seen.

By Tenzin Tsundue

Banned Poem

To die at thirty-five is already too late
you should have been executed in the womb
like your poem   no need
for a sheet of white paper to be your grave

children not permitted to be born
lock up their hands in crime
fingers rot like snakes coiled in winter sleep
eyes rot   escaping the tempest that bites
your face at first touch is a current of water
bones tracing out white scars line by line.

It's a shoal of eels down in the deep water of the flesh,
threading through white seaweed
among still-paler shouts you hear only darkness
coldly wiped clean by another hand
coolly turned into a misprint
placenta wrapping you ever tighter
your last words dying with you

to die today
is to be turned into a stinking news story.

By Yang Lian
Translated by Brian Holton

Forough

I wanted to write a poem for Forough
Knew it would not be published
Wanted to lie about her name
Knew you would not believe me
Believe me
How could I write
So that you would not censor it
When silence is stamped on our mouths
'Believe'
It's emblazoned on the billboards
You can sense Forough's vacant space
And a few lines
Don't you believe me?
So don't publish me at all

By Ali Abdolrezaei
Translated by Ziba Karbassi and Jennifer Langer

2004
Across the Divide

At that time there was no doubt that the Middle East situation relating to Israel and Palestine with its cycle of nemesis and obfuscation and also 9/11 and its aftermath, affected Muslims, Jews, Palestinians and Arabs generally outside the region and not least in the UK. The result was that communication between the groups in the UK was minimal, leading to the demonisation and stereotyping of the other. Myths were perpetuated as the divide deepened and contact decreased. There was also a tendency for each group to construct and select from history according to its own agenda and ideology.

Exiled Writers Ink had a role to play in bringing the groups together to explore narratives, culture, memory, fears and experience through discussion and creative writing. That is not to say that all the members of the Across the Divide creative writing group agreed on every issue, or that writing openly was easy, but the process was as important as the outcomes. Dialogue was always going to be an ambitious aim, but insight into the other was a realistic one, with listening being an important component.

What does all this have to do with resistance? Since the beginning of the second intifada, exiled writers had not only expressed their anger and frustration, but also expressed the desire for peace. Bringing conflicted groups together was an act of defiance against the divide and the participants' willingness to discover 'the other' was equally symptomatic of resistance against entrenched sensibilities and pre-conceived narratives.

By Jennifer Langer

Visions of Peace

The warmth of the sun on cold bones
The sand on bare feet
Trickling in between the toes
You and me, floating in the Dead Sea.

Market traders plying their wares
Chicken, beef, fish
Killed and prepared according to the Law
You and me, feasting with friends.

Olives, hummus and tabouleh
Pita, warm from the oven
Cucumbers pickled in their skin
You and me, a picnic on the beach.

Lighting candles on Shabbat
A family meal on Juma'a
Sitting side by side when peace comes
You and me, enjoying time off.

When peace comes, buses will travel freely
Checkpoints will be dismantled and
Hope rekindled
You and me, curtains drawn inside our world.

By Alex Galbinski

Open Your Heart

These barriers won't topple
A wound comes before another heals

Look at this dark age, enlightened
With the fire of hatred

Are you religious?
Is the source of belief from your land?
Are you the curse of your own understanding?

You were born in war
You grew up on the thin line
Between life and death
You go deep, down slowly
You won't find peace in your own soil
On earth above you
They fight your unfinished battle

Your anger at the fierce cry of a wolf
Your thoughts are sealed
By the hands of a bad day

Open your heart
I know you can love

I'm an outsider with magnifying eyes
In search of wonder.
Mama says religion is the guide
To evolution and humanity
Feed my excitement before I die.
Please.

By Karim Haidari

Salad

On Saturday morning I stood outside M&S.
I was making a salad.
I needed cherry tomatoes, celery, avocados and lettuce.
Camden High Street was busy with Saturday shoppers:
platform-shoe punks, the Jesus Army guy on the corner by the
HSBC bank,
Italians with tie-dye scarves looking for the market.

'Stop', said the woman outside M&S.
Her placard barred my way. It showed bodies bent, mutilated,
scarred, prostrate.
'Don't buy your bread here. This shop imports food from Israel'
I looked at the pictures of Palestinian children
Thoughts of pits filled with other bodies flashed through my
mind.

I felt irritated, resentful.
I was thinking about tomatoes. Which are better?   cherry or on
the vine?

I clung to my anger, held it up like a placard before me and
defiantly
stepped though the automatic doors.
But afterwards I wondered why I couldn't take off my badge of
anger,
which I hadn't even known I had been wearing.

By Rebecca Taylor

To My Enemy

I do not know how to open my heart
to my enemy and take his hand
Tell him never to smile
when he is firing a gun at me.
I cannot hate him then.
If I want to die at his hands
I have to know
whether he is doing it
for his children and his country
or because he has nothing better
to do with the mind of his gun.

By Mir Mahfuz Ali

Reflections

What transformed me into a human rights campaigner were my experiences of travelling and meeting people from all over the world. I realised that our needs are the same the whole world over: the need for food and shelter: the need for understanding, which creates human relations, love and the acceptance of different views: the need for safety and security for our loved ones, waiting to return to a safe and happy life, and planning for the future.

I started to compare my own children's lives and those of my nephews and nieces, and I started to think about what prevents people from accepting something different. I realised that living in London, in an environment where I am protected by one law applicable to all, I had a great sense of equality and security. This is what transforms me and gives me peace from within, and the strength I feel when I address both Jews and Arabs. This sense of inner peace allows me to argue with both sides to rid themselves of victimhood, because both have been victims, and to argue that both sides must recognise the rights of the other, in the first steps towards reconciliation.

I realised how the Palestinians lacked the benefit of my environment, and that the absence of equality is the root of the conflict. It is not just a political problem, but a mixture of all these elements. And yes! The Jewish people deserve safety and security. But it should not be on account of the misery the Palestinians are living in as a result of failure to manage earlier conflict and to prevent us reaching the stage we are in today.

The Across the Divide workshops nourished my soul and I was thirsty and in need of these emotions. I was listening to Leila who wrote a piece about meeting with the enemy. My guard fell away. It is for the young people that I am working. I will go on until the end of the world to create a difference to give that sense of safety and security they deserve to live their lives, in Israel, in Palestine and in this whole world. Yes, I am a woman who has lost her mind and who wants to create a difference and a different world. But I need your help.

By Ahlam Akram

2005
Zimbabwe: Writing Wrongs

Before the Book Café in Harare closed, it provided a space for writers, poets and musicians to perform and speak out. Comrade Fatso is a protest poet who was aware of the dangers of doing so and commented "That's the joke in Zimbabwe – you've got freedom of expression but you don't have freedom after expression." Numerous Zimbabwean writers have been forced to flee and those exiled in the UK, including the late lamented playwright Bart Wolffe and novelist and Caine Prize Winner, Brian Chikwava, have voiced their struggle at our Exiled Lit Café and in the pages of Exiled Ink magazine.

Zimbabwean writing stems from the government's agenda, the 'third chimurenga', the liberation struggle, very narrowly associated with the policy of land redistribution. The 'third chimurenga' bases its creed on 'authenticity', the reference to a pre-colonial past, which paves the way to ultra-nationalism and violence. Numerous writers resisted this state-imposed version of history and some renowned writers fled to live in exile. Chenjerai Hove was forced to leave for being politically critical of the corruption and abuse of power. His defiant poetry collection, *Blind Moon* (2003) was a reaction to the violence which took place with land redistribution. Yvonne Vera depicted female characters who were determined in the face of violence and who defied taboos. She, too, left for exile.

Exiled Zimbabwean writers are engaged in talking truth to power. Mutsaurwa writes about the abuse of power in Zimbabwe and the brutal repression of any dissent, even peaceful protest, leaving rebellion the only option for the people. Mbwembe's poem is deeply ironic, noting that after the battle against colonialism and post-colonialism, comes the final battle against fear itself, fear of the devil you know (the current leader at the time, Mugabe) or fear of the devil you don't know (the opposition leader). Chikowore speaks out about a country driven to starvation and economic ruin by the very leaders it has elected.

By David Clark

The Last Chimurenga

The last chimurenga, the final war
Will it be won, will it be lost
The war of liberty, the freedom war
It's not terrorism but brings in terror
It's not tyranny, that's Mugabe's war
Dictatorship is Mugabe's first born baby
Even the C.I.O. will not come as close

It's unlike the first chimurenga, the Nehanda war
Or unlike the second against the Smith regime
This is the third world war, the final war
The last Chimurenga, the war of all wars
It don't need guns, it don't need bombs

The last Chimurenga is that thing called fear
Mankind faint because of fear
Fear of the known and fear of the unknown
The fear of war, the fear of death
Fear upon fear, will Mugabe ever go
How long will he terrorise us for

Fear of the future after Mugabe is gone
Trusting the MDC to make things bon
Will there be food or much more hunger
Will we be better or continue to suffer
Will jobs be available or worse unemployment
Will there be fuel, will there be water

Which is better, the Mugabe you know
Or the Tsvangirai you don't know
Christians go to church for fear of judgement day
America goes to war for fear of terrorism
Mugabe goes on a rampage for fear of losing power
The fear of fear, will it ever be conquered
Fear…the last Chimurenga, the final war.

By William G. Mbwembe

The Wisdom Herb

Take and smoke the wisdom herb
The way of integrity will lead to suffering
Deep down in the caves of the spirit world
Whoever misses the path will lose their way
In the belly of the earth
Only the true believers will survive.

Greetings, O Great Medicine Man
With the razor that heals the face…
I have a problem I cannot solve
I keep scratching my hives
But they won't go away
So instead I'll now talk.

You have the weapon that usurped power,
That scars us when we protest in peace.
Powerful protest was tried, but we see it has
    failed
Now you lead us, I dare you.
This is the sound of rebellion.

By Biko Mutsaurwa
Translated by Brian Chikwava and Eugene Ulman

Hunger in Harare

The streets are contaminated with chaos
And the black mamba has poisoned the water
Far beyond the reach of consumption
Shops yawn daily with empty spaces
Whilst senseless money is eroded
The land that yielded plenty is now barren
Hunger and thirst shorten lives of many
The end to this now demands the divine powers

By Handsen Chikowore

We Laugh

I wouldn't be here
were it not because
love made me leave
but still
with every heart beat
every breath, every tear
I bleed Africa.
though fond memories heal
there is no pain,
no elation
no escape
from that voice
that is constantly
reminding me
mango trees,
marula
climbing the sgangacha
I'm wrapped in it
on the brink of defeat

trying to find feeling
in their eyes
or dust on their feet.
There's nothing
only the laughter
of my countrymen
in the very face of death
and that sustains me.
How many of these
placed in the same position
would find the strength
or will to laugh.
Maybe that is the reason
we are
Where we are
When we should fight
Or fear
We laugh.

By Hilton Mendelsohn

2006
Forgotten Genocide: Anfal

'Anfal', an Arabic word meaning 'spoils of war,' was a genocide campaign launched by the Iraqi state against the Kurds of northern Iraq. During the Anfal campaign of 1987-88, the military destroyed over 2000 villages, killing 100,000 civilians. Besides conventional bombing, mustard gas and nerve agents were deployed. Thousands were taken to prison camps in northern and central Iraq where men and boys were separated from their families. Most of the males disappeared, executed by firing squad and ending up in mass graves. Women, children and the elderly were held in crowded, unsanitary conditions that caused further deaths. It is estimated that approximately 182,000 Kurdish men, women and children were victims of internal deportation and disappearance. The chemical attack on Halabja in March 1988 caused the death of five to six thousand people. Choman Hardi, Chair of Exiled Writers Ink at the time and herself from Kurdistan, Iraq, organised an important event 'Forgotten Genocides: Halabja and Anfal' which depicted the shocking aftermath in film and words.

For the Kurdish exiled poets, Anfal is a collective and individual trauma that is a deep wound which rarely heals and may fester for perhaps a generation or even more. Yet, despite the pain and sorrow, frequently projected onto the trees, mountains, rivers and stones of the beloved land of Kurdistan, some of the male poets have composed a poetics of resistance – of peshmergas, of martyrdom, of valiant Kurds engaged in a perpetual struggle of liberation, fighting against the powerful military and dying for their homeland. A sense of victimhood is not transmitted because of the articulation of a strong, idealised Kurdish identity inextricably connected to the beauty of the landscape and the fortitude and determination of the people to survive appalling persecution. Such poetry serves to inspire pride and the past and hope in the future and sustains the Kurdish community in their suffering and resistance wherever they are in the world.

Yet more recently the voices of the women survivors of Anfal have been revealed through Choman Hardi's research and her poems in *Considering the Women* (Bloodaxe, 2015). The women's traumatic memories remain present with particular vividness, resisting psychological integration yet the acute trauma, pain and on-going suffering of the women survivors of genocide in Kurdistan is finally exposed in all its horror. In sharing their stories, they unburden their memories, with the poems by Hardi crucially acting as witness.

By Esther Lipton

The Gas Survivor

My body is blooming. Every night leaking flowers,
I turn my mattress into a bed of roses – black,
cherry-red, pink and gold. By day I hand-wash
the towels, recall the stillborn after the gassing.

Who would have thought there are weapons
that turn every part of the body against you?
Every bruise, cough or nosebleed seeming like
the final betrayal? Weapons that turn you into

a despised being in your own village, no one
daring to visit you, thinking you are contagious
Weapons that kill you years after being exposed,
leaving you unable to blame anyone for your death?

By Choman Hardi

Soul Searching

1991 Silemani, the exodus

Watching...
Watching a full-grown proud man
cry, plead, beg
Watching the treasures of the sparkling city
looted by a dirty vacuum cleaner.

Knowing...
Knowing my father would not be
swayed by his younger brother
to leave with everyone. We stayed
Knowing the Ba'athists have arrived
the nose of their tank directed at our house

Watching...
Watching an Iraqi sergeant
search our house and take
my father's precious whiskey bottles.

Watching an Iraqi sergeant look
his way down my sister's curves
Watching the fear
in my mother's shaky eyes.

By Shaee Raouf

The Road of the Gun

I had a small blue sky
The occupiers brought it down over me
I had a little stream of dark blood
a bundle of honey dreams
and a collection of books
they plundered them all

But when they came
to change my skin
deform my face
I wore the snow and thunder
carried my homeland on my shoulders
and took to the road of the gun.

By Rafiq Sabir

Kurdistan

Without you I am without hope or pleasure
Without you I am without breath or whisper
Without you I am without family or shelter
Without you I have neither home nor cover

You are my happiness, my lasting happiness!
You are my angel of freedom, my stubbornness!

Always I will come back to your arms
Always I'll revive the breath of your spirit
Always I will sing the ancient songs of the
             mountains
And sacrifice myself to you, beloved Kurdistan.

By Kamal Mirawdeli

2007
Western Sahara Poetry in Resistance

Suddenly the Western Sahara had come to Bethnal Green London in the form of the Sandblast Festival which was a magical swirl of poetry, workshops, music, and dance in spaces of floating Saharawi fabric and desert tents. Yet the happiness of everyone present belied the sad narrative of the lost Saharawi homeland. As part of the Sandblast Festival, Exiled Writers Ink facilitated two poetry workshops which featured exiled Saharawi poets living in the Tindouf area of Algeria and writing in Arabic, and those exiled in Spain and writing in Spanish.

Morocco's annexation of Western Sahara, after the century of Spanish colonialism started to crumble in the 1970s, robbed the indigenous population of their identity and freedom. The fledgling Saharawi liberation movement, the Polisario, rose in resistance and liberated itself in the south, but the Moroccans retained the main territory, building 2,700 kilometres of walled and guarded defensive structures around this vast area of the desert. The invasion led to the mass exodus of Saharawis towards Tindouf, a small town in the Algerian desert which is one of the most inhospitable in the world due to the aridness and blistering heat. Half the population now lives in the Tindouf refugee camps where the headquarters of the exiled state, Polisario, is based. Contemporary Saharawi writers contest Morocco's occupation of the Western Sahara and the physical representation of that occupation, the Moroccan 'Wall of Shame'.

Many Saharawis consider poetry and songs about their country to be part of their struggle for independence, as they are ways of keeping their identity and culture alive. Much of the poetry is about the relationship with a lover which is a metaphor for the lost homeland. Feelings of love usually relate to yearning, remembrance and being separated by torturers.

The oral tradition played a crucial role in conveying the message of the Saharawi liberation struggle in the 1970s, when most of the society was still largely illiterate. Poetry continues to play a large social and emotional part in the life of Saharawis.

Spanish colonialism and the increased numbers of Saharawis who have studied in Cuba since exile began, have given rise to new generations of Saharawis who write poetry in Spanish rather than Arabic.

By Miriam Frank

Me and You

Now that we are alone
My darling
Which one of us will start
By undoing the other's chains
Whose spirit will be wider
And whose embrace for the other stronger

I.. will tell you everything
I will fill you with myths
And centuries.
I will break your chains before my own
Before the dream is bent
Or thoughts are distorted
And I pledge
To undo my hair
Lock after lock
And present it to you
And any title you give me will suffice in return.

Now with our survival a certainty
Tell me how the rituals go
But first show me:
Your wounds the bars of your prison your shackles
And where your remains are buried.
And I
The lady of past centuries
The glorious virgin
If I was once beautiful

It was because I knew
That my road was leading to you
Shatter me
I long to see my remains
At your feet
My darling..
I spent my life
Creating myself
Into the greatest gift that I could present to you.
I have tried to be a sun
And a moon
That shine only on you
I have tried
To conceal my anger my evil my sadness
And reveal all that would point towards you.
My companion..
I will die or see how you ascend
How stones and harmony
How my blood and your blood flow in your valley
I will die or hear the songs of those who once
loved you
From the heights of your tower
Time
Even twice the time I spent without you
Cannot contain our kisses
For you are a cave within me
And I am the smallest smallest of your symbols
I will deny them all
For you are sublime
Among your rivals
My companion my home
Love and the sword and I
Are verses from your existence.

By Nana Rachid
Translated from Arabic by Nariman Youssef.

The poetry by exiled Saharawis living in Spain, the Generación de la Amistad, Friendship Generation, is poetry of resistance. It is driven by the poets' collective Saharawi struggles as well as their difficult individual lives. The loss of and search for identity often appear as the underlying theme.

We

In this intemperate world we are still
ourselves, those we once were,
those who fight with their bare bodies,
against the abrasive worn millstones of time.
Those who calmed their pierced
chests and bound their hands
over the doves' white flight.
Those who die, are born, dream,
and above all, wait to pull out
from the ashes the identity
of a heart already become fire.

By Saleh Abdalahi Hamudi
Translated from Spanish

2008
Exiled Latin American Voices

Members of the SLAP collective, the Spanish and Latin American Poets and Writers, and of Las Juanas, the Hispano-American Women Writers on Memory group based in London, have produced vibrant performance events of literature and music for Exiled Writers Ink over the years. The poets who are featured here originate from Peru, Chile, Argentina, Bolivia and Mexico and are members of these groups.

In living memory there has been political upheaval in many Latin American countries resulting in years of violence, prosecutions, serious human rights abuses and exile. The suffering and loss of country, home, family members and friends and personal experiences of the terror of torture and imprisonment are shared with others through memory which is dynamic. Moreover, the recounting of memory functions as a means of resistance to counteract definition of the self by others according to their preconceptions.

Both Consuelo Rivera-Fuentes and Maria Eugenia Bravo-Calderara suffered extreme violence during the years of Pinochet's military dictatorship in Chile. The poets' words act as witness and the reader's imperative is to remember the atrocities inflicted in hatred. Despite the difficulty of integrating trauma experiences into narrative, the poets resiliently speak out to resist the idea of victimisation. Enduring the acute pain of torture, Consuelo Rivera Fuentes feels empathy for the suffering of all victims both in Chile and in other countries. Maria Eugenia Bravo-Calderara's poem 'Screaming' is very disturbing too, but is one that she considers represents resistance during torture. In spite of the horrific experiences she suffered due to political persecution, she celebrates life and the redemption found through love and human solidarity.

The Year of the Rabbit by Leonardo Boix is an allegorical poem which focuses on the violence inherent in the treatment of immigrants in Argentina. In *The Dictator's House* by Denisse

Vargas-Bolaños, it is clear that it is risky to stand up against the oppression that was inflicted on the Bolivian population by a dictator.

The writer, singer and musician from Peru, Sofia Buchuck defies the oppression of the indigenous Peruvians in 'People Dancing in the Moonlight' by drawing on her ancestral memory in protest against the suffering of her people. Her poem equally reflects an evocative love of the culture of her Peruvian background.

Resistance comes in many forms. One of the most powerful is through spreading the word, screaming out the injustices wherever they occur, sharing life's experiences so that others may learn, understand, have hope and survive.

By Esther Lipton

A She-River Was Born

Water overflowed under bridges.
Water wept for the Lenka and Miskito people in Honduras
Water howled for the polluted fish in Chiloé,
it screamed for ancient, burned Monkeypuzzles
in Lonquimay, Wijimapu and Pikúnmapu in the South of Chile.

Water cried, wailed and sobbed for the poisoned
Quimi and Chuchumbletza rivers
and for the Shuar community facing death in Ecuador.

Water gushed out down her legs, flooding mansions,
huts, *Rucas* and houses, drowning pets and people
merciless dragging them,
enraged,
along with stones, torn tree trunks, leaves and broken branches.

The deluge of her body was final and deathly.

There was no water,
only flames and faces with no names in Grenfell Tower

because water was watering the gardens of the wealthy
                              across the street.
There was no water for her in Syria; only bombs
                              drying out her tears
and Hamad desert burning her eyes.

There was no water for me in that marine room of blue eyes
                              and blue uniforms of blue light,
of blue electricity shattering my blue body
and diluting it in aquatic nightmares.

I wanted to drink from the Mediterranean Sea, from the Pacific
Sea,
from the North and South Seas
but ended up with my mouth full of salt…
Silent, mute…

After the horrific wind
had torn away her house, doors and windows,
water gushed out with swirling fury
from her womb
and dragged dogs, cats, horses,
jaguars and rats
who, with their panicked eyes, rushed to nothingness,
desperate to survive.

It rained, rained and rained
and at the end of the warm rain
PACHAMAMA gave birth to this
SHE-RIVER of women who
weaves resistance and
rebellion.

Our birth cry was
REVOLUTION!

By Consuelo Rivera-Fuentes

People Dancing in the Moonlight

I saw you my people
Dancing in moonlight
Dressed in red
Blood of innocent Indians.

Your wound
The exploitation
The loss
Of your children

I need to paint your hopes
To dance with you in the wind
With the reason to exist
To keep alive your colours.

People of the Amazon
Lungs of the world
Dressed with pearls, sapphires and emeralds
With gold and silver.

Wild flowers on your head
Warm hands of brotherhood
Your jewels of secret legends
Not yet defiled.

Sweet perfume of lilies
Mountains of corn and quinua
Dressed in icy skirts
Rivers and sea at your feet

I saw you my people
At the frontiers of man, waiting to see the far end
Grasping to understand their ownership
Hanging the sky with both hands.

I saw you my people
Hanging from the thread of life and death
Singing water cascades
And dancing as no one had ever seen.

By Sofia Buchuck

The Dictator's House

I remember the steep road
leading to Avenida del Libertador,
uneven cobblestones.

I remember the deserted bridge,
a warm white glow pierced
the night icy sky.

I remember el río Choqueyapu,
the burble of the stream
carried silenced dirt.

I remember hands clutching
the bag, cans of red paint inside
like bells announced my steps.
I remember Virgen de Lourdes Grotto
illuminated by green traffic lights,
incandescent shadows, the three of us.

I remember long seconds of rattle
in unison, red letters hissed
at the guilty wall.

By Denisse Vargas-Bolaños

The poem refers to an infamous general who ruled Bolivia as a ruthless
dictator in the 1970s, returning in 1997 to become the democratically
elected president of Bolivia.

The Year Of The Rabbit

After Mariano Peyrou

Even though you didn't leave
because of a knock at the door
you promptly returned
as if coyotes were after you

twice thrice crossed the border in Summer   you made
few holes   there were
cow infested meadows   a southerly beach filled with crabs
where to hide   an orphan's treasure
the idea there was something beneath the surface

There was a black and white lighthouse, and a ship-wreck being
eaten by glowing anemones

wood was your only element
but burnt it all   left a small pyre
of charred letters   books in Spanish   badly knitted scarfs
a hollowed boat in the shape of a sister
that didn't want to follow
beneath every sea is another sea is

you   crossing the ocean   Rabbit's weakness:
hesitancy   *The Bible says*   you're so lucky
hat your flower   the fragrant plantain lily
is the common hosta   *siempreverdes* shared with blue slugs

Undomesticated Leporidae   no selective breeding
but a tree line that will end with you
          the house began to fill with   rabbits   *conejos*

& their short memory
as they emerge in *primavera*
from their well kept burrows
after the last snow is almost gone
and predators are on the hunt.

By Leonardo Boix

Screaming

Another scream rips the night
and a scarlet tongue
drips blood from the sky above.

In the darkness
a dazzle of evil stars
are blinking.

Like a nightmare
the air carries human screaming
and then another shriek.

Wounded animals, howl
lashing out at life
and everything that still remains.

The screams echo
filling all the world's night
with pitilessness.

Then all that exists
rocks.

It is the Apocalypse.

It is the end of the world
under the scarlet tongue,
the entrails,
the bodies hanging
from a sky that drips with blood
like a gigantic slaughter house.

In this place
the torturers wear the star of Chile
on their uniforms.

Here they administer pain
and death and tell me
I must prepare to die.

Distant cries of children
being tortured
tell me this is the end of the world.

As if I were gravely ill
or at the point of death
I realise I have lost everything.

Every last hope.
I stretch out my hand fumbling
desperately for god's finger,
anything, any little bit
of god or his shadow.

But I find nothing.
My soul is a heap of ashes
burnt beside me.

I gather them up as best I can
and as if I were really dying,
I put them on.

Next day I am ready
for further torment.

By Maria Eugenia Bravo-Calderara
Translated into English by poet Dinah Livingstone

How to make your balaclava?

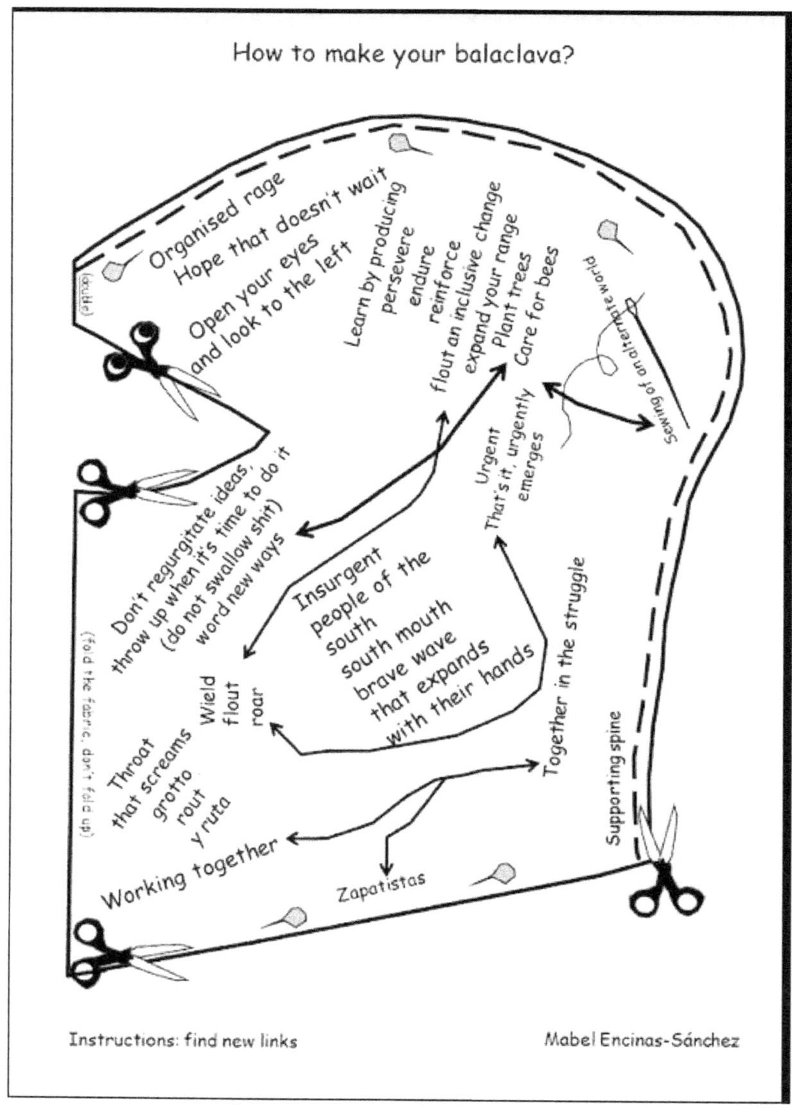

2009
Writing Home: Remembering Bosnia Herzegovina

In 2009 Exiled Writers Ink staged its theatre production 'Writing Home', a play performed in bomb-scarred Mostar and Tuzla in Bosnia Herzegovina. It was produced by Exiled Writers Ink committee member Edin Suljic, himself exiled from the part of former Yugoslavia that became Bosnia Herzegovina. Directed by Ernst Fischer and written and acted by exiled and non-exiled Bosnian writers from Bosnia and London, the production brought together writers of different religions, ethnicities and cultural backgrounds and those who left with those who stayed.

The Yugoslavian war came from the old religious and national divisions of that country and, at the end, resulted in its disappearance. New countries were formed based on those religious and national differences. One of those newly formed countries retained its religious/national mix, becoming a smaller Yugoslavia, in all but name. That is Bosnia and Herzegovina. The war has stopped, but the divisions have stayed.

How does one 'Write Home' if one has abandoned it years ago, running away from a war, ending up in London? Equally, how does one 'Write Home' if that home was damaged, and one was forced out it?

And so, to start with, two writers supported by Exiled Writers Ink, escapees living in London, Amna Dumor, originally from Mostar, and Edin Suljic from Tuzla, went together to their old towns to team up with writers who stayed there, surviving the Yugoslavian/Bosnia and Herzegovina war in the towns of Mostar and Tuzla, to create a performance based on their writings about the war as each of them experienced it. The project turned out to be about resistance to nationalisms, paradoxically in the midst of old divisions and still present wounds from the war.

The divisions in any society run deep, even when they don't turn into violent conflict, they are always visible. At the same time there are people everywhere who reach across divides and who seek reconciliation after the conflicts.

Edin was able to reach out to and rely on old friends from the times when they were all living in Yugoslavia. They had remained internationalists, even when the borders around them were redrawn and new divisions created. They are the people who still carry the brunt of the sectarian divide left after the war. And while Edin and Amna were able to return to the comfort of the Western world, their old friends stayed within the divisions, where tribal loyalties are still so strong.

Eventually, they created a performance, in each of those towns that would span across the centuries of Yugoslavian/ Bosnia and Herzegovina complexities, culminating in the last war. But also they were able to tell their own individual stories, about pain and loss, their own stand towards national and religious divisions.

They resisted tendencies to forget each other, to blame each other for the war, to lay claims on who had more rights on victories and defeats. They were 'Writing Home' for each other. And then they parted. Those who stayed would have to resist nationalisms and separatism. Those who came back would have to resist the complacency of the Western World, keeping bridges suspended through writing.

The whole project was an act of resistance to the events of the past thirty years: the exploiting of old Yugoslavian differences, amplifying divisions, resorting to war as a means to rearrange the geo-political set-up of that part of the world, the continuation of supporting national and religious sectarianism and promoting further separations and intolerance. 'Writing Home' was an antidote to all of this.

The work in this section all explores similar themes of loss, displacement and identity and ultimately, the ways in which the act of writing enables the victims to resist succumbing to overwhelming grief and the destruction of war.

By Edin Suljic

Assassins

They follow my every step. They know me well.
All my mistakes, all the things I loved.
They know all my secret shortcuts.
They turn up at the right corner long before I get there.
And I don't try to run away.
How could I? After all, I too know them well.
I fed them. I got drunk with them night after night.
We sat around a table. I looked into their eyes.
I held their hands. Some I kissed.
Many I held in my embrace..
And I betrayed them, many a time.

So I wait, knowing they are waiting.
I hope they will come out of the shadows.
But they don't. They won't come closer.
They wouldn't let me smell their perfume
or inhale a wisp of their cigarette smoke.
Like this, we remain forever locked in; they
who never leave me, I, who never let go of them.

Most of all I fear you, my love.
You know every hollow under my skin
You know when I breathe out.
You could stop my heart with one touch … but you don't …
You just lay there at night, next to me, under our blanket,
encircling every bend of my body.
There we remain forever in waiting.
I, who is waiting for your kiss, for a blow,
and you, who are waiting for my hope to fade away
But the blow doesn't come and the hope doesn't fade.

By Edin Suljic

The Year is 1992

The year is 1992. Still vivid in my memory, I see my dad playing chess in the courtyard during the short cease fire and my mum going about her usual business of preparing dinner. There is a deserted street, a simple reminder that nothing is the same anymore. I imagine suddenly being lost in my own town, my own life. The air is filled with that special smell, a nostalgic smell, which is usually associated with memories of childhood, the first kiss and first love. All those memories are now slowly diminishing in the presence of overwhelming fear and uncertainty, threatening me with oblivion.

Leaving my hometown, I observe the distant lights and the heavy red clouds hanging over my beloved city. I notice the buildings disappearing behind a wall of dust, and then the curtain drops – everything is invisible. When I finally open my eyes, a road stretches ahead of me. I am lost again and I wonder: "Who am I if my heart and my soul are not with me? Have I left myself behind and where is this road taking me, to nowhere or to new beginnings and a new life?" I shall find out and I will – who knows – maybe – some day – return.

By Amna Dumpor

Spotlight on Elvedin

I am called Ragib and once upon a time I was a stonemason. It is already the three thousand nine hundred and sixty fourth day that I am like this, a monster and a cripple, dying slowly in my own body and at the hands of one who is secretly disgusted by me – my wife Vasvija. A landmine cut off my legs and mutilated my body, so I'm blind in one eye, as well as mute.

I am called Ragib and I rarely leave my house. My thirst for other people stopped long ago. An old pen with a mother of pearl cap is my only link with the rest of the world. I speak through it and thus distinguish myself from the dead silence of objects and walls. With its help I can be what God is not allowing me to be – a human being. I am Ragib

Light off on Elvedin, light on on group
Various voices: Here I … I … I … I am … I … I … I am
… I am a plural noun
Light off on group, light on on Elvedin

I am the one on whose window sill a flower wilted this morning. I have one eye left, but have no tears to water it; a well inside me has dried up and so, though it has been given to me to suffer, I am forbidden to cry.

Yes, I am called Ragib and you must have heard of me if you have ever walked down the alley. I don't know how to speak, so I write down what can't come out of my mouth. I don't go anywhere and I don't show myself to anyone, that way my pain is smaller, since it has not been touched by others.

My name is Ragib and since I became a cripple, I have not dreamt. I am not afraid to go to sleep, but I am afraid to wake up; and like that – forever – one of my eyes looks into this world and the other into the World Beyond.

I am called Ragib, the one whose wife cheated on him yesterday. During the war I lost my legs, but in peace I grew horns; don't ask me if I know which curse lies heavier on me.

I am called Ragib. I am a stonemason, who cuts words with his hands – words of stone.

By Elvedin Nezirovic

Sticking to my Soul

Sticking
to my soul: a worn-out dress,
a knight's armour,
is growing ever heavier,
becoming unbearable –
deceit.

Somewhere
behind, hidden and far away,
I am barely breathing –
waiting, doubting.

Between
the two of us, desire signals
for one of us to stop –
existing.

I am taking off my tired
dress of life;
a thousand masks fall
to the ground.

My soles are still white
despite treading hot sand
toward the sun
I wanted to go

I have left

By Sonja Juric

2010
The Power of the Pen:
Ethiopian Exiled Writers

London based poet Alemu Tebeje was forced to flee from Ethiopia in 1991 because of his opposition to the regime and his support for Gebreyohannes (aka Gemoraw), one of the Ethiopian literary giants who was a poet expressing the agony of the Ethiopian people and calling for freedom. Gemoraw was executed in 1991. Tebeje continues to resist in exile, not only through his poetry and journalism, but also through his website campaigning which includes co-administrating a website named after Gemoraw. Hama Tuma is an exiled Ethiopian political activist, a poet and writer who became an advocate for democracy and justice. This has caused him to be banned by three different Ethiopian governments.

There is strict censorship in Ethiopia whose media environment is one of the most restrictive in sub-Saharan Africa. The authorities continue to use lethal force and repression against those who protest, including writers. Fear of retribution by the Ethiopian government also negatively impacts on the distribution and production of work by Ethiopian writers in exile. Recently four London Ethiopians were insistent on their real names not being used when they performed a poem for BBC Radio Four on the theme of Homer's Odyssey. In fact, the poem was about a student leader who demonstrates against a Cyclops dictator and is forced to flee from his country.

Alemu Tebeje turns to humour and rage to fearlessly tackle difficult issues such as corruption and injustice. His heart remains firmly embedded in Ethiopia and through writing his poetry and lyrics he situates himself there. Faced with the world's indifference and iniquity about Ethiopia, Hama Tuma expresses anger and passion in his poems of protest and hope.

Exiled Writers Ink was honoured to be invited to speak at Alemu's book launch of *Greetings to the People of Europe* at the Poetry Café, London and to celebrate Hama's book launch of *Just a Nobody* at Keats House, London.

By Jennifer Langer

Visa

The chairman in a woollen suit and tie
and expensive buffed shoes
flourishes *his Charter for Peace and Democracy*,
touts the ethnic fairness of his government,
words like

Human Rights!
Growth and Development!

slip easily through his lips,
he is happy to repeat again, again
the changes ushered in over the years,
so generous with talk, talk, talk…

eventually he throws the meeting open
(even if his eye does not like questions)
and the first enquiry floats up
from one of many young protestors
thrown into Birsheleko, a boy whose t-shirt
shouts

NEVER AGAIN!

whose legs are plugged in ragged trousers,
one shoe smiling through a hole in front
but twisted at the back, his other foot unshod
and swollen, broken by a whip.

This boy gets up and says:
"Mr Chairman, I have listened carefully,
but with respect I feel that everything

about my life is different to yours,
Perhaps I live in another country,
Are there two Ethiopias?
If so, I would like to leave the one
where I have been and visit yours.
Do you know where I can get a visa?
Is there someone with an application form?"

A moment's laughter brightens up the hall.
but the boy is only tightening his chains.

By Alemu Tebeje

When We Return

When we return
        one day tomorrow,
when the exile ends
and loneliness and despair vanish forever.

When we return
        let us hear the music
of love and hope renewed, not hate.

When we return
        let us not visit
the mass graves and cemeteries
but the museums
the nurseries of happy kids.

If and when we return
        let it be to
the future we'd dreamt of.
died and sacrificed for,
not to the past
so much abhorred,
nor the present loved by no-one.

When we return
        let it be
to the tomorrow we died for.

By Hama Tuma

2011
Hostile Environment

In 2012, the United Kingdom set forth a series of immigration policies designed to make life as difficult as possible for anyone without leave to remain or settled status. The right to work, the ability to find adequate housing or to claim any sort of benefits or help from the state were whittled away. These policies had a devastating impact on those hoping to claim asylum or refugee status, leaving many in an unlivable limbo of poverty as they awaited decisions on their applications, which were under increasing scrutiny. The journey of so many seeking a new beginning in the U.K., free from the persecution of their homelands, is now a journey that too often ends in detention centres that increasingly resemble prisons, while thousands of others fall through the cracks of a failed policy.

At the heart of its work, Exiled Writers Ink has always tried to support refugees, asylum seekers and those in exile to find ways to share their experiences with the wider world. The difficulty of being forced to flee from one's home country in hopes of a better life, only to be met with hostility, fear and aggression. The increasing criminalisation of immigration and the profound impact this has on one's mental and emotional wellbeing is a theme that permeates and in this chapter, we explore concepts of displacement, isolation, anger, but also the ways in which one can and does resist despair and finds hope.

In the wake of Brexit and the rise of far right populist movements across the world and the tides of xenophobia and nationalism sweeping the globe, it is now more important than ever to continue to share these stories, these experiences, as a means of resistance to our increasingly divided times.

By Danielle Maisano

Life in Corridors

Left, right, doors close
In front, behind me, they shut
Doors slam, slap the chipped out
Plexiglas click-closing, sleek 'n' smart
Some, slide-slapping, just in time
Sensors detect, deter the chipped

Rushing towards the slapping, no chance
Doors without handles,
Digitised, programmed, well groomed
Privileged access and I'm not accepted.
Doors, I hear what you're not saying.

Scanning doors, decide my fate,
Scan my history, not my brain,
My capabilities, you can't scan these
Your sensors know who and what to welcome.
Doors, you shutter my dreams.

They clap-close, so apt, shun me,
Squeak close, bar me, ban me, swing me away
Expertly, silently.

By Nkosana Mpofu

Tenancy

The landlady led me
into the upper storey,
the December evening
pressed against
the uncurtained windows
inside the bare silence
thudded on the wooden stairs
I placed my hand on the banister
desperate for support
the cold wood electrified
but the old apparition
kept on mumbling
about tenancy,
as if the palest of the script
the bedroom opened,
suspended in the dank English smell
oddments of the last Christmas,
the false impressions
hung in the wallpaper—
it was like boarding
the wrong ship
but I signed the deed
and on my way out
near the brown hedge
spaces warned
but I held on
and dislodged the bags.

By Rizwan Akhtar

Defeated but Not Broken

They disperse you
to out-of-London locations
Into towns ripe with
racism and unwelcoming communities.

They cut you away
from all those you know
They deny children their fathers
They give you Section 4 support
For food and toiletries
£5-a-day to live-on
No fiver for a winter coat
No fiver for a decent
pair of shoes
No fiver for a day out
on a summer day.

£5-a-day in vouchers
A 30-minute walk
to the supermarket

By O.T. Mukozho (Otilla Tsvegie Slater)

2012
Words for the Silenced

Poets, journalists, activists and artists are gathered in the basement of a crowded London café to celebrate and to acknowledge the work of four brave men imprisoned across four different countries for their words and efforts to speak the truth. The evening event 'Words for the Silenced', was hosted by Exiled Writers Ink and Amnesty International UK, not only in an attempt to show solidarity with the imprisoned writers, but also as an act of resistance to the increasingly censored times in which we live. The freedom of the press and the freedom of expression that were once seen as pillars of Western democracy seem to be slowly eroding all across the world, emboldening the most oppressive regimes to imprison, murder and persecute journalists, poets and artists of all forms who dare to challenge the ways in which we view power.

Since its foundation, Exiled Writers Ink has been dedicated to campaigns against such injustices. Another event was hosted in partnership with PEN Norway to raise awareness of the dire situation of the poet Ilhan Sami Çomak imprisoned for twenty-six years, his only crime a chance meeting with a Kurdish girl he barely knew who had a sibling in the outlawed PKK. Continuing to write poetry, coupled with the excitement of knowing that people outside, like us, are reading his lines far away in the free world, helps him to continue to resist and to endure both mentally and physically.

In this chapter, we feature work from Ilhan Sami Çomak alongside the work of two other writers featured during our 'Words for the Silenced' event. Ahmed Mansoor is an Emirati poet, blogger and human rights activist who was arrested and sentenced to ten years in prison, accused of posting false information on social media which "insulted the status and prestige of the UAE and its symbols." Galal El-Behairy is an Egyptian poet and lyricist who was imprisoned in Cairo in March, 2018. He was sentenced to three years in prison. His charges include blasphemy, spreading false news, and abuse of social media networks all due to his poetry and the lyrics of the song *Balaha* which is sung by the Egyptian rock singer Ramy Essam.

The men that were honoured during both events, like so many countless others, are journalists, poets, bloggers, and activists. At the time of writing, they still sit in prison cells in the UAE, Saudi Arabia, Egypt, and Turkey. While these men continue to resist, continue to write from their prison cells, we must continue to help their voices to be heard.

By Danielle Maisano

What Are All Those Stars For?

What are all those stars for?
And the night
And the clouds
And the sky erected like a tent in the desert
In a place like this
Everything is
Luxury

By Ahmed Mansoor
Translated by Tony Calderbank

It is Getting Dark

With the tongue of a great snow
Your name is written on mountains.
Maybe cliffs open their doors
To you and others as you walk.

It is getting dark.

After sun in the caves of the light
You know sweat swells drop by drop on
Your face; will pollute faster than an eye's blink.
It is getting dark.

Yes, it is getting dark
Even for my question.
Which hangs in a world of butterflies, or
Trees fast among aged purple sycamores
in lakes deep and black in myth?

Light may turn and turn again
In our minds. We knead bread.
We need night's uncertainty blurred
It's an unsharpened knife,
A knife to give blood its due.
And your voice rising,
A stream of resemblances.

Waterfalls steal music of gardens.
A little storm breaks.

By Ilhan Sami Çomak

The Tartan Shirt

Tora Prison - June 27, 2018

Your letter's tucked away
in the sleeve of a tartan shirt:
it flies towards you
and greets you.
Yet I fear that if they searched that shirt
it, too, would become afraid
and forget how to speak.

I fear that as soon as they set it free
it would run away, promising
never to return.
Then it would be just a shirt – nothing more.
Forgetting its ID,
it would walk slowly among the masses
and be ambushed
and stripped of its dignity
by His Eminence
who would do it harm.
It howls and cries… but who is there to call to?
"Help me, world! For shame!" it yells.
Then the officers start beating it,
and some might even
loosen their belts. And so
that venerable shirt of mine returns to prison
and is accused: "Enemy
of the state."
I'll write your letter:
It will either reach your door
or remain in the shirt
and be lost.
…..

My dear young lady,
my loving rose:
It is to you
that the prisoner writes,
surrounded by soldiers,
soldiers everywhere.
He greets you
and misses you –
you, a song carved on walls,
you, the caravan of ports,
of doors,
the jailer of the man
who is a part of you.
You, the one who blocks the ears
and suppresses the truth
and denies the call to prayer
until all that's left
are the claws of ghouls
crushing all hopes
and burning all dreams.
All that's left
are the waterwheels groaning
and a thieving, toothless fox.
But all that's needed
is a bit of faith
for your daylight to return,
for you to be fertile and green again,
for your fire to scorch
the cowards' nests.

/continued

I hope your health returns, you beauty –
you, the last old woman
and the first young lady
in the eye of time.
In the end, I'll love you.
As a prisoner, I'll love you.
As a free man, I'll love you.
Even when you stubbornly oppose me,
still I'll love you.
So ends the letter
of your lover, the prisoner
surrounded by soldiers –
soldiers everywhere,
soldiers and walls.

By Galal El-Behairy

2013
Iranian Women Speak Out

A now notorious example of the ongoing crisis of human rights in Iran was the case of British Iranian Nazanin Zaghari-Ratcliffe, stopped at the airport in Tehran after visiting her parents; she was detained by the authorities and separated from her infant daughter. Soon afterwards, she found herself in prison. She became the latest and most visible member of a large community of the arbitrarily imprisoned in Iran. The centre of an international outcry, and the subject of a campaign spearheaded by her husband, Richard Ratcliffe which has garnered over three million supporters' signatures – as of this writing, she remains a prisoner.

Zaghari-Ratcliffe's plight became the inspiration for an 'Agit Lit' evening of poetry, activism and soul-searching. For the event, EWI joined forces with human rights blogger, Simone Theiss, Amnesty International and Howell Productions, a dynamic young theatre group.

The first half of the evening centred on a play written by the Howell company based on transcripts and interviews, telling the story of Zaghari-Ratcliffe's imprisonment and its impact on her family, particularly her husband, Richard. The play was long listed for the Amnesty Freedom of Expression award, noted as 'political theatre at its best'. At the Poetry Café, Richard Ratcliffe was in the audience, and spoke to the packed room afterwards. Movingly, he reminded the audience that Nazanin and other women imprisoned alongside her were aware of the event taking place and that they knew their words and stories were being heard. During the break, audience members were invited to join the Amnesty letter-writing campaign on Nazanin's behalf and given materials to continue to campaign.

The second half of the evening was devoted to readings from Iranian women writers. EWI member Nasrin Parvaz read from her memoir, recounting her own eight-year imprisonment in Tehran. Poet Ziba Karbassi, former Chair of EWI, gave a characteristically electrifying performance of her work. Finally, Simone Theiss read poems that had been gathered by Richard Ratcliffe from Nazanin and other writers imprisoned with her. Originally published on her CiLuna blog, the words of the silenced ended the evening.

Sadly, women are still being held in terrible conditions in Iran's notorious prisons. Many are only guilty of standing up for human rights, like Nasrin; some have become part of an elaborate game of geo-political chess, like Nazanin.

From the bottom of the dark well of their experiences, their words rose and will continue to rise, like a butterfly beating against the hide of a rhino: Ephemeral and fragile wings that may one day yet cause a storm of change and justice.

Below is *an* extract from Nasrin Parvaz's *One Woman's Struggle in Iran, a Prison Memoir*. Here, Nasrin describes how she became politically active, and how she first saw the net that was about to close around her.

By Catherine Davidson

Chapter 1 - Arrest

Tehran, 13 November 1982

I was twenty-three and I'd just started to feel I had a purpose in life. Like so many of my generation, just after the Shah was toppled I'd joined one of the groups opposed to the new Islamic regime…

War came when Iraq invaded Iran on September 22,1980. It changed everything for the worse. Khomeini used to say the war was a blessing, a divine gift. I only understood what he meant later on; because we were at war, no one could make demands, not even for food, and the Islamic regime could get rid of all the people and groups who wanted a secular government, freedom, justice and equality.

I was living at home and my parents knew I was attending political meetings and demonstrations. They saw my copy of *Towards Socialism* and all my other socialist books and pamphlets. They became increasingly worried.

'Be careful!' they always used to say. Yet I don't think they really believed I was putting myself in any real danger. At first I didn't either. On TV, the Islamic regime's newscasters talked constantly of the arrest and execution of armed fighters, terrorists and traitors. I wasn't armed, and I didn't see myself as a traitor. All I was doing was talking to workers about the need to organise and struggle for employment rights.

Yet in 1981, I was shocked out of my complacency when Ali and some other friends of mine were arrested and executed as traitors and infidels. All they had been doing was printing *Peykar*, a socialist newspaper. After Ali was hanged, his father came to Tehran and visited us. He told us that before he was hanged, Ali had been beaten to such a total pulp that when they showed his father the swollen, purple, faceless corpse of his son, he had not recognised him.

It was really only when we heard Ali's father that my parents and I fully realised the danger I was in.

By Nasrin Parvaz

Writing Cells

What thread of rain can we hold onto   not to let it fall
there is no tear here for your teargas   brother
and nothing of blood to pour down the gutter-runnels a little bit
                          south of the east of us here
cult of the body-gobblers in the formality of gorged cities
the swollen corpses of the dead under Shogholle are witness
our dead ones are being shoved under the table
& news of it as tongue-torn as ever
                          between the teeth of white lines

/continued

& every media hung in dumbed formation &with each belch
                              you can smell the blood
like a cloudburst on a napping street handcuffs of the
disappeared,
                              blocked bridges, blocked roads
my keenings have more edge than all those words
more blood-dark than their bomb-nights the morning call to
prayer
words that try to avoid walking start to dodge bullets & zigzag

breaking of voice-sounds shrieking   & at the end
                              ooohf it can kill
I us
us Iran
with all its borderlands, its little corner-lands
we with our wounds
wounds that go in deepest at home
I us
all of us   people & breathing & drrmm drrmm drrmm
drum-filled & bomb-full (& bom bom bom)
our hands are emptied of guns our throats
                              are stuffed with bullets
I us
us Iran
we with our wounds
wounds that go in deepest at home
& corruption as ever comes from commerce & scamming &
scabbing,
        from market-bazaar & hanging tree
hubble-bubble toil & rubble   not to work works better than
all their babble
what can we hang onto   not to let it fall
there's no tear here left for your teargas brother
they have threaded our blood vessels   to gas pipelines
boiling boiling blood-bubbles   break the fasts of morning
so, we give you Iran
voice of revolution

Revolution   revelation   revelation

           revolution   revolution

    revelation   revolution
   revolution

      Revolution !

By Ziba Karbassi
Translated by Stephen Watts and Ziba Karbassi

The following poems have been published with the permission of Richard Ratcliffe and the Free Nazanin campaign.

Couples in Prison

You are under the sky of the same city
Just a little bit farther
And a wall between us
As deep as a hand span
We drink tea without each other
And shape clouds in our dreams together
We experience not being with each other
And together we watch the trace of migrating birds
Our date will be
kissing the first star
That twinkles at us every night

By Golrokh Iraee

Autumn Light

The diagonal light falling on my bed
Tells me that there is another autumn on the way
Without you
A child turned three
Without us
The bars of the prison grew around us
So unjustly and fearlessly
And we left our dreams behind them
We walked on the stairs that led to captivity
Our night time stories remained unfinished
And lost in the silence of the night
Nothing is the same here
And without you even fennel tea loses its odour.

By Nazanin Zaghari-Ratcliffe

Not Seeing You

For Richard from Nazanin

Not seeing you was enough
And
All this torture
The dark and small cell
And the wall of stone
Is for what?
Not seeing you was enough
For the world to become a cage
And I
A lovebird alone
Breathless, with a broken heart

By Mahvash Sabet Shariari

2014
From the Camps

While this chapter was being written, a boat bearing the work of artist Banksy was out in the Mediterranean, rescuing migrants at sea, and trying to draw international attention, once again, to the crime against humanity occurring just outside Europe's borders. The pink prow of the Louise Michele garners temporary attention, while countries close their ports and we all collectively close our eyes. One more story is added to the hundreds that mark Europe's failure to help vulnerable refugees seeking shelter at its borders.

Creativity itself can be a form of resistance, sharing it, performing it, enabling it. Like other organisations, EWI resists Fortress Europe, through teaching, workshops and highlighting the words and art coming out of the camps. Two events illustrate this ongoing work.

On a cold night in December 2018, EWI hosted a remarkable event at the Poetry Café: a live-linked simultaneous reading showcasing three young Afghan women poets living in Athens. The poets call themselves the Plaza Girls and are a collective of teenage girls who found themselves in Athens in 2018, having travelled from Afghanistan, Iran and Turkey. On this evening, the poets appeared live, reading to an audience in Greece, watched by an audience in London. It felt as if both groups were joined in mutual witness. After hearing the reading, audience members were able to discuss and ask questions. Homan Yousofi, a poet who had worked with the girls in Athens, was in London to translate and facilitate. With the help of a grant from EWI, the Plaza Girls published a magazine of satire, haiku and analysis based on their experiences in the Moria camp on Lesbos, Greece. Their booklet of poetry in English, *Chink of Light* had been beautifully produced by Homan and both publications were available on the night.

Now living in a self-organised anarchist community, the Plaza Girls work offers a different view of resistance, one where optimism and action is pitted against despair and indifference. The girls spoke with power and confidence – and their voices were heard and applauded.

Their escape from the camp and ability to find a voice in a new language was a reminder of another EWI attempt to resist the ethos of Fortress Europe: a trip to the Calais Jungle camp in 2015, the year before it was demolished. At its height, the Jungle held 8,000 refugees, waiting in limbo between France and the UK. Many British citizens responded by offering aid. Even after it was destroyed, these acts of resistance and solidarity continue with those who have made their way back.

On that occasion, six poets from EWI: Fatima Hagi, Firdos Ali, Husam Eddin Mohammad, Salam Kidane and Shabibi Shah - from Somalia, Syria, Eritrea and Afghanistan – visited Calais. They performed their work in the languages of the camp and donated bilingual books to Mary Jones, who had set up the Jungle Library – a visionary effort to offer the solace of books and friendship to those stuck in a hard place.

This chapter ends with an extract from the memoir of a Yazidi artist. It is prefaced by Nazand Begikhani, whose work focuses on resistance to gender-based violence. Art, poetry, even satire, help artists forge identities beyond victimhood and towards power and agency.

By Catherine Davidson

From Chink of Light

the following are excerpts from a long poem

Continent of borders
  the prisons of mindsets
  makes bright suns sets

Dead dryland of borders
  eyes drowning behind
  tear the chains
Break stony walls

The wings of this girl
  take strength in flight
with her mountain brothers glide

Bad and good move on
  like the blossom bow
pine tree cleans my soul

Destroy the chains
  drown them in the sea
make the depths speak again

Wind like breath
  sun makes table still
juice becomes sweeter

I am waiting for when
  the dark corner inside
  will set itself ablaze again

By The Plaza Girls

Beyond Victimhood: A Yazidi Voice from Sinjar

The Black Hands is the life story of a teenage Yazidi girl who survived terrible atrocities at the hands of ISIS after their attack on Sinjar in 2014, including forced displacement, captivity, torture, forced conversion to Islam, forced marriages and sex slavery. Sohaila survived several suicide attempts not only during her captivity, but also after her liberation and return to the IDP camp of Sharya in the Kurdistan Region of Iraq.

The force of her resilience and resistance found echoes in art and self-expression through a creative art project initiated by the University of Bristol in cooperation with local artists, NGOs and humanitarian agencies. Sohaila is another example – like Nadia Morad, who reached beyond victimhood and became an actress – of a rising young artist who now works with an NGO helping children with disabilities. Her paintings are regularly exhibited in local art events, where people queue to purchase them and have her signature written in henna on their wrists and palms. The story is part of a collection of narratives entitled *Shattered Hopes*, produced by internally displaced women living in the camps in the Kurdistan Region.

The Black Hands

Finally the black hands got us; me, my mother, father and my siblings. Unfortunately, we didn't succeed in escaping the ominous day when the force of destruction took our secure city, Sinjar, by surprise, the city which was sleeping kindly under the sky of God.

I am Sohaila, 18 years old. I wasn't lucky enough in education or in life. I only had the chance to study up to year four in primary school, which at least made me literate. On 3 August 2014, when history recorded the imprint of shame on the face of humanity, me and my family were squeezed into a car hoping to escape our reality, just the same as the other families. However, we were not lucky, as the car broke down in the middle of the road and we had to continue our journey on foot. So we became an easy target for ISIS who captured us and returned us to the city.

In the city the ISIS forces separated the men from the women and children. Later on, they killed the men and made us prisoners of war. We had no choice: either death or submitting to Islam. I knew nothing about my father and siblings; their destiny was unknown. I was forced to submit to Islam and utter the *Shahada* (Islamic testimonies), without understanding a single word. Thence, a *Sheikh* had come into the room and asked me to repeat some words and then he spat into my mouth. From his point of view, I was now considered to be a Muslim girl.

A few days passed and I was taken to another place. It was a huge hall with different kinds of methods of torture, including intimidation, starvation and beating. I remained not knowing anything about my father and three brothers. I wonder what happened to them, had I lost them? Had they been killed? Would they come and rescue me? Days, months and years passed and I had stayed a prisoner for three years. They sold me eight times to various men of whom I knew nothing about. Every one of them had treated me according to their moods. They took their anger out on me and started beating me, bullying me, forcing me into starvation and tearing my body like a wild dog.

The first time they had sold me to the governor, who gave me an ID card. Then he sold me to a man from Baghdad, and then to a man from Tel'afar and finally he sold me to a man from Mosul. The situation went on like this until I could not differentiate between them, as evils don't differ from each other. A very stringent surveillance system was put around me so that I would not be able to escape or get out and talk to others. There was no mobile phone, no nothing. I was not allowed to see my mother, except with surveillance once every nine months. I had no choice except death. Therefore, I tried to commit suicide twenty times by different ways. I had diabetes and blood pressure tablets whenever I got them. I tried to strangle myself and cut my veins so many times, but I was faced with failure every time. After each suicide attempt, they began to starve and torture me more and more, giving me only a small handful to eat and some water for long time.

After three years, the Iraqi army had come closer to the city of Mosul. This situation led to a state of doubt and uncertainty among the ranks of ISIS. The man whom I stayed with tried to take me to Syria across the border. Through some friends I managed to contact my family. My friends helped me to tell my family of my whereabouts. Finally, I managed to get away from the terrorists by the help of a network secretly deployed by the office of Prime Minister of the Kurdistan Regional Government, Mr Nechirvan Barzani, who had ransomed me back by paying the sum of $6800. I remained with an Arab family from Mosul until Iraqi forces and the Peshmerga entered and liberated the city. After a few days my uncle came and took me with him.

At that time, we wanted to reach the Kurdistan Region by any possible means. However, for security and safety reasons the Iraqi forces stopped us from doing that. They were on alert to attack ISIS. In the end, we managed to leave Mosul behind and reach Sharya camp in Duhok city. There was a huge number of displaced and rescued people from the violence of terrorists in the city of Duhok. I arrived at the camp feeling down and having severe pain all over my body as a result of the torture and barbaric rape by the terrorists. Worse than this was the news of my father, three brothers and nephews being missing with no one knowing anything about them.

In the camp the humanitarian organisations took responsibility for taking care of us. They arranged rehabilitation courses and psychological treatments so that we could get over the terror and coercion with which we were faced by ISIS, and help us forget the stress and pain of what we went through. I took a course in drawing in spite of knowing nothing about it. To a great extent, my teacher gave me a hand in learning how to use the brushes and colours, until I was able to draw many portraits. I love drawing so much and I participated in an exhibition which was held in the Sharya camp. I am so keen on drawing now and don't want to give it up, certainly wishing to learn more and achieve higher skill levels.

That is my reality. Life goes on and on and I cannot forget about what has happened. Up to this moment I cannot forget my missing father and siblings. Also I'm not able to get rid of memories of the wild acts of terrorists and what they did to us. I love and thank everyone who took part in rescuing me from these filthy people. I really appreciate the help of friends, families, also humanitarian organisations which rehabilitated me psychologically and have sown hope in my heart. My thanks also go to those who support projects inside the camp. I wish these courses would be continued, especially variety arts, which was carried out by the University of Bristol. We are in great need of such courses which help us develop our skills psychologically and artistically.

By Sohaila Ta'lo
Compiled in Arabic by Beyar Muhamad
Translated from Arabic by Zekra Zahawy
Edited by Dr Peter Greenhouse

Dearest Trump

Dearest Trump, you sweet almond,

Your blond hair like the falling leaves in autumn. Your skin glittering like the warm glow of fried pilau rice. Your body as wide as a great oak. We hope your food will always be warm and your beer served cold.

From your own hand on Twitter, it's always said that you are the greatest president ever. We follow you. We are here in Europe. Here they crush our rights under boots. Believe us, in these matters, Europe has been worse than Afghanistan.

Arriving at Lesvos, we found that all the media: the newspapers, television, films and radio were reporting a bunch of lies about Europe's hospitality. The camps show their real hypocrisy. You are more clear and direct with your hatred. But in Europe, where they brag of human rights and welcoming people, we see the true conditions in Moria and how they treat people. But we know that you are always telling the truth, with your porcelain smile and those sweet little hand gestures. Of course a picture of tolerance, with your wives from all different countries. Europe promised us a lot of things but it has so far been all fluff and meaningless. Now the responsibility rests on your neck.

Wishing you all the success you deserve and not a drop more!

By the Plaza Girls

2015
Syrian Writers for Love and Peace in Syria

In a show of defiance in their call for peace in protest against the war in Syria, the title chosen by the Syrian writers for their Exiled Writers Ink literary activism event was 'Syrian Writers for Love and Peace in Syria'.

The war in Syria on writers did not start in 2011 but in 2000 when the Assad regime took charge of Syria and tried to suffocate all writers. According to Haitham Hussein, the Syrian novelist exiled in London, dictatorship oppressed the writer preventing him/her from telling the truth about despotism as this revelation would disturb the status quo imposed by tyranny. Therefore writers in Syria are subject to silence or imprisonment, caught between following and supporting the dictatorship or writing covertly. The writer in Syria feels in exile within the country before actually being physically exiled, because of political, social and religious obstacles, the main one being political. For Hussein, the writer resists and overcomes these difficulties through the solidarity of sharing work and expressing his thoughts to ease his pain and bring peace to his inner soul.

What the war added was a higher level of oppression and suffocation in the form of arbitrary imprisonment without trial and in many cases, summary executions. As a result many writers went into exile while others stayed their ground and fought with their pens as weapons until they died.

Those who fled into exile found in themselves a sense of loss of home and belonging. Thus, these themes started to emerge mixed with struggle and resistance against the war and the people's suffering. Malak Mustafa, an exiled Syrian poet, describes resistance and struggle, which includes nostalgia, as a constant throbbing wound in her hand that is impossible to ignore. What is evident is that the writers are insistent on their own voices being heard to resist generalised media narratives. Exiled Kholoud Charaf's annoyance about the media gaze on Syrian suffering, immediately forgotten by the viewer, is palpable in her poem. She felt helpless in the context of war but in exile writing and painting have enabled her to survive as a human being healing herself and, in the process, also helping others. Exiled poet, Amir Darwish, is intent on determining his own narrative which counters stereotypes of refugees.

Finally, Malak Mustafa sees the struggle as universal, and not only Syrian, given that the pain of one human being should be all humanity's and so she exhorts all poets to unite to stand against tyranny, despotism and dictatorship so that human dignity triumphs.

By Jennifer Langer

Their Knives

Their knives,
Those knives piercing our bodies
Weren't cold like the strangers' knives
Our brothers!
On their hands
Our blood mixed
With our blood
And as severed limbs
We shivered
In that intimate stabbing.

By Nada Menzalji

Photo

We take pictures of the air swallowing us
So the world can see
We take pictures of a cat gnawing our bones
So the world can know

We take pictures of how the ant died, how it
                        became drunk-headed and fainted away
To annoy the world

88

We take pictures to keep suffering awake
                        so it stays away from us
And the world turns away from it
We take pictures with a vintage Panasonic
How children go hungry
So the world's appetite is fed

We take pictures so that I see and he sees and you
    see
But only the camera sees
Who says the world has eyes or time to see?

Don't worry. We'll be a little angry,
Our feet and tears will scuff the earth,
Our consciences will tremble and we'll replace
                        one foot on top of another
And our souls will shudder
But the world will soon change the channel

Ton upon ton of us have died.
One child drowns
And suddenly the world sees.
It is a bit bothered
And nobly saves a few
And we forget that we were created human
And all this earth
For our brief lives

Is ours.

By Kholoud Charaf

We Want To Live

On a margin of a forgotten camp
With pain we want to live
With sadness
With agony
With traumas
We want to live
With or without food
We want to live
With thirst
With enemies or without them
We still want to live
Under a cut in a tent with every drop of rain at
      night we want to live
We want to live
At the long queues for clothes we want to live
With every step we take towards the journey of
      death
We want to live
With every tree we pass
With every pride swallowed, we want to live
With or without our children
We want to live
With or without our parents
We want to live
We want to live, simply because we love life.

By Amir Darwish

Where I Come From

From the earth I come
To the earth I come
From the heart of Africa
From the kidneys of Asia
From India with spices I come
From a deep Amazonian forest
From a Tibetan meadow I come
From an ivory land
From far
From everywhere around me
From where there are trees, mountains, rivers and seas
From here, there, from everywhere
From the womb of the Mediterranean I come
From a mental scar
From closed borders
From a camp with a thousand tents
From shores with Alan the Kurd I come
From a bullet wound
From the face of a lone child
From a single mother's sigh
From a cut in an inflatable boat about to sink
From a bottle of water for fifty to share
From frozen snot in a toddler's nose
From a tear on a father's cheek
From a hungry stomach
From a graffiti that reads, 'I was here once'
From another one on a tree says 'I love life'
From a missing limb
Like a human with everything I come to share the space.

By Amir Darwish

Memories

I miss our house
Placed on top of the mountain
Between the fog and summer breeze
accompanied by the shy rays of the sun.

I miss my mother's smile
And sipping coffee with her
I miss putting my head on her chest.

It's the memories of summer
that will never return.

By Malak Soufi

I Came from Syria

A handful of sand
The wind's embrace
What is hope but others' attempt
to hold on to life,
like we did.
Life is the last source of water spotted in a desert.
O Son of Adam,
The heart is a bomb
and you, a suicide bomber
unaware of when the trigger will be pulled.
I once believed
I was a citizen of the world
My sense of belonging has been constrained,
It closed down upon me.
I am the victim
The mortal,
I came from Syria

By Nada Menzalji

2016
Out of Europe

Writers who were European Community citizens responded to the results of the June 2016 Referendum with passion.

The largest group amongst the three million EU citizens living in the UK were Polish (850,000) who bore the brunt of negative attitudes towards Eastern Europeans perpetrated by some individuals and local populations. Brexit allowed interpretation of the referendum results as endorsing their exclusionary views and seemingly gave them permission to be abusive and overtly racist. This was manifested in their accusations that Poles and other Eastern Europeans took jobs from British people and put a strain on public services such as housing, hospitals, schools and welfare. The animosity extended to racist and extreme xenophobic violence towards Poles.

Brexit had a devastating effect on some Eastern European writers who articulated their feelings of anger in resistance to this xenophobia. Yet this sensibility was mixed with despair, sorrow and fear. Maria Jastrzębska states that her poem 'June 2016' was written out of the utter despair she felt at the referendum result, along with all its racism and xenophobia, and her attempt to climb out of that. 'Also - deliberately - it's an un-English tree... I wanted to write an angry poem but wrote something more in sorrow than anger, though I did and still do feel plenty angry!' Anna Blasiak writes too, about her anger, but is also aware of a new atmosphere of fear. Bogdan Tiganov, originally from Romania, has made Britain his home. His poem illustrates his fruitful multicultural personal relationships before Brexit and his acute disappointment at the values that led to Britain leaving the European Union.

By Esther Lipton

June 2016

I've heard that cypresses point
folded hands towards the sky
in prayer so thought I'd ask this tree
which stands close to the edge
of the water and is naturally tall
though still young judging by the tuft
of untidy new growth at its peak
which being thinner sways a little
in the wind while the rest of the tree
is upright entirely motionless
under the slow lights of a plane say
and even though I don't believe
in anything I could explain I thought why
not ask the tree to pray for me for us

By Maria Jastrzębska

A Friendly Fishmonger in the Harbour

A friendly fishmonger in the harbour suddenly spews TV-hatred
                            as acrid and thick as toilet bleach.
His fish spoils faster.
I go vegan.

People are lighter
in the streets, ready for flight.
There is no looking each other in the eye.
Dense fear mutes
the tongues of other languages.
And then there is the "oh, we like your lot, it's the others..."

I can still see the coast of France
when the air is clear.

By Anna Blasiak

Rowan

I know you.
I know you so well. And
yet… Jarzębina czerwona,

your red berries –
jarred conserves,
strung necklaces or songs.

You were always
so very cheerful. But in this
country you are not

a children's tree
but
witches'.

Your smoke –
druids' telephone line
to the nether

world. Your wood –
a shield against
lightning and thunder-

storm. Your whisper
in the harbour –
its armour.

And I don't know you.

By Anna Blasiak

The 1st of January 2021

My first good friend was Turkish –
we understood each other through play,
and he gave me a watch that played a tune
but I lost it at the swimming pool.
My second good friend was British –
he had a haircut like Damon Albarn,
and soon I spoke the language of
Shakespeare, Keats and Wilde.
My best friend was Libyan –
we loved each other's cultures,
Christian and Muslim brothers
sharing God's food.

I don't recognise this country now, this hatred,
this apathetic nationalism, this resigned fear.
It's lacking in sophistication.
This is not the Great Britain I loved,
of culture and tradition, and taste and class.
We've been consumed by Americanisation,
big business, selfishness, dumbed down rubbish –
swallowed it whole with a Diet Coke.
Seduced by the good life, we turned our backs on
culture and embraced propaganda.
So, here we are.

Alone.

By Bogdan Tiganov

2017
Let My Dreams Laugh: The Uyghurs

The persecution of the Uyghurs has evolved into a more genocidal policy despite the mantra 'Never Again' following the Holocaust.

The Uyghurs are a separate and distinct Muslim people who had sovereignty over Xinjiang state for many centuries. However, in the 1980s and 1990s there was a brutal denial of their human rights by China. Subjugation, forced assimilation, discriminatory and oppressive policies resulted. Uyghur resistance, both physical and intellectual, calling for a form of nationalism, (cultural unity either as an independent group or a regional group within the larger Chinese nation) have according to China, justified its action to oppress the Uyghur people and turn Xinjiang into a surveillance state.

Currently, it is estimated that there are about two million Uyghurs detained in so called 'vocational training centres'. Human rights violations, such as arbitrary arrests, imprisonment, forced labour, organ farming and murder, have escalated. Women are subjected to rape, forced abortions and sterilisation. Hundreds of poets, musicians, and public intellectuals have disappeared in an effort to silence and eliminate Uyghur cultural thought.

With increased repression, forced assimilation and cultural genocide, the need for the Uyghurs to have a voice of resistance is urgent. To quote Rahima Mahmut: 'Though living in a free country, the UK, since 2000, my mind is not free from the atrocities that are occurring to my people and country.' Ever more fearful of their voices being silenced and their culture and religion being eradicated, Uyghurs resist in exile by speaking out in poetry and narrative to enable their voices of protest and testimony to be heard. Simply telling others and spreading the word about how disappearances and atrocity affect the emotions is resistance.

Hendan's poem 'Returning to Fire' reflects a re-awakening of a desire to 'go back and suffer with my people.' Though exiled in Turkey and having lost contact with most of her family, she feels that 'being dead in one's own land is better than being alive with a strangled soul.' She feels helpless to help her own people. To write and to share poems about feelings of depression and loneliness is but another form of resistance.

Two Exiled Lit Café events featured Uyghur poets and musicians. In solidarity with the struggle, the emotion of the listeners was palpable in their response to Aziz Isa Elkun's poetry, Rahima Mahmut's singing and the music of the SOAS Silk Road Collective.

By Esther Lipton

Borders

15 February 2019

How long is it
since you became a source of conflict?
We all know well you did not exist
before Adam was born
At that time humans were kind
and they knew how to love
So why did humans create you?
Why are they obsessed with you now?
There are so many wars because of you …
You know
Trump's war of the wall with Mexico
Putin's border war with Ukraine
Xi Jinping's borderland war with the Uyghurs
Erdogan's border war with Syria
Britain's border war with Europe and so on …
So why do you wage war over borders?
No border, no power has the right to
Take away our God given rights

We were all born to live free
I want all humans to be free
I want the millions of my fellow Uyghurs
Set free from China's internment camps
I am ashamed to see caged humans inside your walls
I want to break your cage
I want to break your silence
I want to be free
Free like a bird
Like a wild pigeon
To fly freely in the blue sky
Because we all have only one world.
No time for war and fighting!

By Aziz Isa Elkun

Returning to the Fire

February 2019

I will return to him,
Return to them
My eyes can't sleep anyway
I see a night through all my days
Down my fingers my stars are seeping away
I will sit beside him and close my eyes
Let the dark dungeons have their nightmares
Let my dreams laugh by their side
Never mind, let my arms be tied
As long as it is not my heart being burnt again
Whips, please slash my face
My strangled soul cannot take any more
The noose is about to break

/continued

Don't cry if you hear the news of my passing
Say the cold, the hunger, the thirst
And the crisis of identity
Set me free

Cast the stones from your heart
Don't give me another thought
It is my hatred for sobbing that will buy the ticket
It is my hatred for weeping that will pull my luggage
It is the mourning that will seize my heart
That will release my veins, relax my fears
When the black bag over my head shouts
Ürümchu
It is just my burial shroud running for my mum's tomb
What ease to go back like this
With cruelty to grant my wishes
Before the final death
When you hear the strange news "He died"
Say "He is not dead".
How can one die in the soil of one's homeland?
His only duty now is to smile
Clinging to the bright, white earth that has been
          his home all the while.

By Hendan
Translated by Hendan

2018
On the Front Line and Towards an Open Land

Over the past few years anti-Semitism and Islamophobia have reared their ugly heads in earnest. These are challenging times for both Muslims and Jews with both groups on the front line facing fear and hostility and framed as the guilty 'other'. Fuelled by social media, venomous racism has come from both the Left and Right. Muslims and Jews were attacked verbally and sometimes physically, and at the very least, tended to be stereotyped and scapegoated.

Our 'Towards an Open Land' project was created as a means of enabling Muslim and Jewish writers to provide insight into the complexity of identities to resist hostile narratives and to be in conversation about the issues that affect their lives and creativity. We turned to poetry in our Nottingham workshop, which was part of the Changing Wor(l)ds Festival, where Muslim and Jews came together in the solidarity of shared vilification and resolve to present their own singular narratives. The series of London creative writing workshops that followed complicated simplistic Jewish Muslim divides by drawing on the participants' experiences and cultural backgrounds to create work that rejoiced in difference and diversity. We intend to take our project on the road in England to draw in local communities to interactively expand the range of stories and our conversation and to engage with them as allies in the struggle against racism.

By Jennifer Langer

Beyond the Veil

My modest dress that you see
As a sign of oppression
Is for me the symbol of ultimate liberation

It urges you to look beyond the veil
To peel the skin
To peep through the physical
The limited, the confined
Straight into the essence
The infinite, the boundless

It's a glaring statement
I am more than just a body
I am a mind, a heart
And a soul

Don't just stop there
At the door
Come in
Get to know me
For what I really am

It gives me contentment
And great satisfaction
With my femininity
It gives me dignity
I refuse to be portrayed
As a sex object

It gives me freedom
To choose my dress
Not only wearing what men desire

It gives me protection
From all undesired attention
For my intimacy I only share
With the one I love
Does that make any sense to you?

By Nahida Yasin

Khundal Khon

was my great great aunt, a poet, who declaimed
to the Court of the Emir of Boukhara. Not a
    concubine
(she married in her time and went to live in
    Jerusalem)
but his solace, she would stand and recite, all day
    long.

A commentator, a weigher of words, a Jewess
with the ear of the Moslem potentate, whose
    command
was absolute and whose subjects deferred in every
    regard.
Did she flatter him, did she offer insights, was
    she veiled?

By Yvonne Green

Rickety House

7.6.2016

The wind sweeps across this morose land
dangerous forces shake the rickety house
now she hears the venom she can't stand

Ranting and roaring they are not banned
the hate trolls emerge and quickly pounce
and the wind sweeps across the land

Their verdict is guilty and be damned
her vision in the cracked mirror screams and
        howls
as she hears the venom she can't stand

In her body the wounding arrow brands
the hate trolls bang their drums aroused
and the wind sweeps across the land

She'd dreamed of utopia, of a glorious land
she'd wear beads, adorn herself with flowers
but she hears the venom she can't stand

Now her resistance has been fanned
let the trial of the anti-Semites commence
still the wind sweeps across this land
still she hears the venom she can't stand.

By Jennifer Langer

Halvah

You held my hand
as we shopped together,
the *deli* with sawdust on the floor,
open barrels of sauerkraut,
shelves with jars of preserve,

dark glossy mysteries
winking with their delights.
A conversation bubbling
high above me
where the marble counters lie,

the offer of a gherkin,
a treat, descends from a tall jar,
the pleasures of its sweet
and sharp vinegar burst
after my dull school dinner.

Treats from your other land,
I gazed up at boxes of halvah.
Would we have enough money?
Was today a special one?
I gripped your hand very hard.

Helva, halvah, halwá,
I wished that box into your bag-
a heaven into my belly,
those squares of sesame
soaked in honey.

By Stephen Duncan

Festival

They claim back their street.

No cars, no hoots,
no traffic warden, no trace of bullets.

Music invites me to spin, I oblige,
Surrounded by hundreds of dancing pumpkins

Is it new for Beirut?
It's new for me
New for the blood donation team
And flocks of happy Filipinos
Holding potato crisp kebabs
Irresistible falafel aroma too

A nine-year-old girl with painted face
Says Hello

By Anba Jawi

2019
Eating from the Turkish Restaurant:
Poetry and Resistance in Iraq

Resistance renews itself with each generation. This has been an era marked by astonishing creative mass-protests – in Lebanon, Chile and the United States young people have been at the forefront of the marches calling for their rights, sometimes even dancing for them.

In October 2019, Dr. Anba Jawi, a poet in the Exiled Writers Ink network, alerted the organisation to a series of extraordinary events taking place in Iraq. An ongoing series of protests against corruption and cronyism had drawn in thousands of young people to Tahrir Square in Baghdad. They had set up camp and formed an alternative community– a site of permanent protest. The camp seemed utopian – complete with free libraries, volunteer medical care, shared meals, street art, music – and poetry.

The protesters were young, inventive, optimistic, and under threat. Their insistence on democratic transparency had drawn the ire of the ruling regime. Subject to harassment, kidnapping, and tear gas attacks, some protesters had canisters fired directly at their heads; many died. The protests gathered around a central icon: the derelict former parking structure known as the "Turkish Restaurant."

The poems that follow begin with a celebration of the Turkish restaurant" and its message of solidarity. They are a selection from a December 2019 EWI event at the Poetry Café. Translations in English were read by London drama students along with original poems read by the poets themselves by video link. A live broadcast shared the work with over 1,000 listeners. The poems continue to find an audience around the world.

As Safa'a Al Sarai, killed in 2019, puts it here 'A poem is a letter made of fear, loaded onto a dove's wing, fragile but still able to fly.'

By Catherine Davidson

At the Turkish Restaurant

I wanted to ask for one dish of joy
The waiter came
And the restaurant cook
And the accountant
The driver came
And the local old beggar woman
Street vendors came
And night guards
The homeless came
The tramps who rest
at the bottom of Al Umma garden *
Motorcyclists came
And tuk tuk drivers
Even bullets, smoke and heartbreak came
And the river
And the bridge
And the tunnel leading to Aljumhuria Street **
Many things came
Humans, rocks and trees
With dirty clothes and swollen eyes
Even that Iraqi God we know came
He had not slept for many Octobers
I was baffled, and asked him:
I just wanted to ask for one dish of joy
We turned together
Baghdad was filling the bowls of all who came
Washing their faces
Bandaging their heads
And shaking the cradle
of those who sleep in eternity   **By Maitham Abdul Jabbar**

*   National Gardens next to Tahrir Square where the demonstrators camped

* *   One of the streets that ends in Tahrir Square

Small Eyes Heave

Small eyes heave
Stationed at home base
Small eyes flee from
Small heads
Glue to my mouth
Their eyes in my mouth
Mother
Their eyes stuck to my brother's trainers
Their heads are small
Enough for half a bullet
To crumple
Their noses are soft and definite
I will hang them on the fridge
And forget them
Their feet move on their own
Walking in the street
Entering dirty hospitals
In new ripped jeans
Their feet erupt onto
My shirt soaked with slogans
Their shiny hair pukes on
A wall full of graffiti
They have small shoulders
Mother
Shoulders that eat their backs while dancing

By Nour Darwish

I Should Have Died

I should have died
Smothered by smoke
Or been run over
Or been shot by rubber bullets'
Careless assassins
However I live as an old worm
I eat and watch and laugh: a betrayal
And I know my profound
Loneliness as well
I return to my disappointment today
Friends died who were younger than me
If I shall live
Oh my hand spasms shame
To write stories about my friends!

By Amer Al-Tayeb

Our Sun Has No Earrings

Our sun has no earrings
Our sun has no braids
When our sun without her bracelets dims
Our sun and the reeds curse
while the guard falls asleep
to the sound of water

Our sun is lost in the garden
sleeping too much with the wild rice
We wait for her the next morning
Our sun, it's hard to say
has no place in our thoughts
Our sun is not like any other sun

We loaded the wings of the doves with vows
A heap of promises on every bird
Letters written on paper made of fear

Our sun aches in the night
Naïve, we didn't know how to fly
Naïve, we didn't know how to rise up
The cycle of our naivety goes on too long

O friend, O Swayhb, O that deep wound
I glimpsed you in the distance
Put the saddle on your broken heart
And let's go on

You, like a date,
You who refused to die
Our sun aches in the night
Plait her braids, put on her bracelets
And let's keep going

By Safa'a Al-Sarai

A Kiss is the Distance

A kiss is the distance between two lips
Ready to embrace

And blood opens the window to impossible apocalypses
Teardrops scratch the ceiling of ancient memories

The soldier is within a bullet's distance
And the bridge extends its arms in Al Tahrir Square

My broken voice
No, no
Bounces back stained with love
Sprouting green space
Creating you and creating the world's
New song

The rain drizzles me
Perforates the umbrella woven from thick smoke
Punches the head of memory

A jester pulls the trigger
The rifle farts and life ends

Ayad Al-Qla'ay

2020
Black Lives Matter

The Black Lives Matter (BLM) movement was born out of a struggle, the plight of a people to be treated with dignity, civil rights and to receive fair treatment as citizens under the law. In 2013, as a response to the acquittal of Trayvon Martin's murderer, George Zimmerman, three American women Alicia Garza, Patrisse Cullors and Opal Tometi started the social media hashtag #BlackLivesMatter. Over the past several years, that hashtag has grown into a Black-centred, modern day civil rights movement and political project responding to police brutality, unjust imprisonment of Black people and all forms of institutional racism. The movement is known for organising mass protests across the world and calling for an end to police brutality and racial injustice.

In 2020, footage of the very public murder of George Floyd at the hands of American police officers in Minneapolis began circulating on social media and news outlets. The world was once again woken up to the harsh realities of police brutality and systemic racism. During a global pandemic, thousands of people took the risk of marching in the streets of major world capital cities; from Washington, D.C. to London, Paris, Berlin, Stockholm, Rio de Janeiro, Johannesburg, Nairobi, Toronto, and Buenos Aires, people rallied in solidarity with anti-racism activists, with the BLM movement at the forefront of organising the resistance. Once again #BlackLivesMatter was trending as many sought refuge in speaking out against racial injustice on digital platforms.

In July 2020, Exiled Writers Ink, in solidarity with The Black Lives Matter movement in both the UK and abroad, and in support of those protesting and fighting for an equal and more just society, organised a sold-out online poetry event on the theme Black Lives Matter Through Poetry. The event featured poets from the U.K., U.S. and Canada and was attended by a diverse audience, logging in from all over the world.

While much of the attention over the last few months has focused on events in the United States, Exiled Writers Ink recognises that the institutional and structural racism seen in the U.S. also exists in the United Kingdom. The brutal history of British imperialism and colonialism has resulted in the oppression of Black lives and its impact still reverberates throughout our society and institutions to this day, with the recent injustice experienced by the Windrush Generation being a stark reminder of the institutional racism that still exists in Britain today. BLM is very much a part of the larger puzzle of resistance movements across the globe. With the aim of organising consciousness, whether expressed through online activism, mobilising in the streets through peaceful protests, advocating for diversity and fair representation in the arts and showcasing work through literary activism, it is our duty to fight for a better world, free of bigotry and all forms of injustice and inequality.

Throughout the ages we have seen Black literary voices using their positions of influence to educate and bring to the forefront the ugly nature of racial inequality. The writers whose work you find in this section may be contemporary in nature yet if you take a moment to delve into the essence of their work you will find echoes of a past and present interwoven so closely it is almost impossible not to see how very little has changed.

Poets Tessy Aura, Tshaka Campbell, Simone Yasmin and Fatima Hagi, featured in this section, have used their writing as a form of resistance to counter systemic racism, imperialism, neo-colonialism, patriarchy and challenge attitudes towards race in the US, United Kingdom and Africa. It is vital that the Black Lives Matter movement is not an isolated resistance struggle, but is very much connected to all forms of oppression that people who identify as Black, experience both perpetrated by the state or by individuals, irrespective of which country or continent they may be living in.

For instance, when in the poem *'Genesis'*, Tessy Aura reflects on the remnants of colonialism in her home country Kenya, one must understand that these are the same remnants of colonialism experienced by the refugee girl arriving in the UK who is subjected to anti-immigrant sentiments. In her poem 'I Heard It, But My Heart Felt It', Simone Yasmin eloquently writes about racial microaggressions, which for many Black people, are just as harmful and emotionally draining as the overt racist slants that they may receive by white supremacists at an anti-racist protest. Similarly, in the poem 'Wild Hair' Fatima Hagi talks about what it means for someone to make comments about a Black woman's hair, although this can be seen as a harmless remark or perhaps unconscious bias, it still has a great deal of psychological effect on the Black women who are experiencing this on a daily basis, and for many of whom it is a form of discrimination intertwined with racism.

The poems presented in this section are not only an act of defiance, but a remembrance of those lives and identities lost to police brutality, imperialism and racial inequality, Tshaka Campbell pays homage to the young man killed whilst jogging in his neighbourhood in Georgia, in the poem 'Ahmaud Arbery'. We can see here that Black writers use their pen to immortalise the dead, so their names are more than hashtags in a fast-moving digital world where it is so easy to forget and move on. In these poems we are reminded that fighting for a different world is not only a worthy cause, but necessary to survival for people who identify as Black.

By Fatima Hagi

Genesis

She carries dead bodies on her head like a turban.
More like a leso wrapped around her head to balance
                    what's left of our legacy,
She holds her head up high skilfully,
Trekking for miles,
Back breaking,
Exhausted,
But still dripping with pride,
Because, here,
She knows no other way,
Here.
She still has borders to feed,
And corruption to weed,
Here.
No one is going to ease the burden off her neck or her back
                    without an interest rate attached.
Here.
The Internet won't stop for her because in the race to develop
                    there is no time to grieve,
No time to wait for apologies and condolences.
But don't be fooled by her humility.

----She is the mother.
She is the genesis.
Slit anybody's wrists,
And you will find traces of her;
Evidence that more than once,
In a muddy hut,
In the presence of lions and elephants,
She copped a squat.
And at 11.7 million square miles dilated,
Greatness slid out of her thighs,
And into the palms of the Savanna.

Dipped and baptized in the Nile,
We were set free to roam the endless plains of the Serengeti.
That is the truth I wish the history books would reconcile.
Back then there was no questioning the connection,
Or the origins, the proof was in the melanin,
The sun rose and set on it,
And everything it touched,
Her offspring controlled.
And every time we leave to try and make fathers
                    out of lands unknown,
She permits the exodus,
Begrudgingly yet secretly hoping for it,
Because the prodigal child always returns home,
With a greater love for it,
With a deeper understanding and appreciation for
                    the fabric of their identity,
Knowing that it is their lifeline;
The umbilical cord that unquestionably links us all back to her.

By Tessy Aura

Ahmaud Arbery

What would you do if
dropped into the middle of a prayer
where both ends lead to purgatory...

you'd run
run like the ends
were burning toward center soul
And in this state of faith
kneeling would turn your everything
to black smoke and eulogy
you'd run
even though your mind would tell you
to "hold on" to the prayer
but this scripture reads
"guilty before conception" so
immaculate is a "fugitive" blood type

...run
cuz you are a phenomenon
a dogma
a "slave" to what should be freedom
as is what God poured into Eve
before the serpent made visible
what bare skin means to the world

you'd run
to where the walls were built
with fractured hands
already familiar with broken

where you were authorized
to be sacred and
could rinse your body of its own master...

and like far too many

you'd meet this promise land
as a dead church
waiting for its caskets to fill
with runaway black boys

By Tshaka Campbell

I heard it, but my heart felt it

Everyone always mentions the microaggressions,
Those fetishes and strange obsessions,
But my first encounter wasn't subtle.
See, the harsh consonants beat the air from my lungs,
The words hung heavy in my little 8-year-old mind,
As I was pushed aside at lunch,
And told 'you can't sit here…because you're black'.
And my little tabula rasa mind was struggling
                              to decide and codify,
As you tried to deny my presence.

9-year-old me was greeted with gollywogs at a friend's party,
2, 4, 6, 8 sat side by side staring down at me from the stairs.
'They're just collector's items', the mother said,
And she watched my Black eyes flicker at
                              the sound of her white lies,
Knots formed in my stomach.

At 10, a friend and I begged our teacher to celebrate
                              Black History Month.
We had fried chicken, bakes and plantain,
And when tasting our food, they got a taste of our culture,
And like colonisers what they liked they kept.
Vultures coming for the culture, but never the pain,
Wanting our style, but not our delayed start to the game,
So, in 2020 I know I'll still have to ask workplaces to celebrate
                              Black History again,
I think my children probably will too

So, for me, it was blatant, blunt, obvious,
But then came the microaggressions.
See, all the overt stuff stops,
Or maybe you just get used to it,
But you never stop feeling it.

And suddenly racism came packaged in little parcels
                    and tied with ribbons.
You know those boomerang compliments like:
'You're pretty for a black girl' or 'you look like you can sing',
And even, 'your hair doesn't feel very niggerish'…
That one made me wince.

And whilst their fingers interlocked through my locks,
                    I filled with dread.
For once annoyed that they didn't ask that question,
That I've heard far too many times.
That they didn't ask my consent,
Didn't ask my permission,
Before invading my hair, my safe spaces and home.

Every day, I wake up black and every night I go to sleep black.
And yet, on Monday I'm told I 'sound white',
But on Tuesday I 'sound black' again,
Then on Wednesday, I'm told to 'stop acting black',
But on Thursday, you think I need to 'stop acting white',
And every damn Friday I'm interrogated with
                    'where are you really from?'
And on Saturday, your eyes pierce mine as you interrupt with
                    'no I said REALLY from?'

And on Sunday's,
On Sunday's,
On Sunday's I sigh,
I cry
I grieve
I struggle to breathe.

By Simone Yasmin

Wild Hair

"Your hair is wild", he said
I took a step back for a moment and pondered on
                    this wild hair of mine
Do you mean wild as in unruly and difficult to confine?
Like the slave girl who ran from her master till she was
                    dragged in the mud by her hair
Wild like the chains that weighed my descendants to
                    the bottom of the sea
Wild like Lady Day singing Strange Fruit in complete darkness,
                    with no encore
Only to land herself in prison for 366 days

"I didn't mean it like that though", he said,
"I meant wild like fun and exotic!"
Fun and exotic like when Sarah Baartman was exhibited
to gratify a hungry gaze and meet their wildest fantasies
The black Venus stood naked and exposed
Prodded and poked like a science experiment
"She's exotic" they said, "We haven't seen anything like it!"
I'm sure it was fun to have wild thighs and exotic hips
Consumed to the bone
To tame and untangle
every piece of the history
that lives in every strand of my hair
Till the follicles no longer give birth to melanin pearls
wrapped around every curl there is memory you see
twisted and coiled tightly so I don't lose parts of myself
So yes, my friend, my hair is wild and free! *Raised fist*

By Fatima Hagi

Reference

Contributor Biographies

Ali Abdolrezaei is a poet, writer and political theorist with over seventy books. In Iran he was known as one of the most innovative poets of contemporary Persian poetry. He is leader of the Iranarchist Party which has played a major role in the fight against Iranian Islamic dictatorship in recent years. Abdolrezaei left Iran in 2002 after protesting against the censorship of his books *So Sermon of Society* and *Shinema*, which led to him being banned from teaching and public speaking. Abdolrezaei's poems have been widely translated.

Rizwan Akhtar is from Pakistan. He studied in Britain and is now Assistant Professor in the Department of English at Punjab University. His poems have appeared in *Poetry Salzburg Review, Poetry NZ, Wasafiri, decanto, tinfoildresses, Postcolonial Text, Poesia* and a few have been anthologised by Forward Press UK.

Ahlam Akram - Born in Nablus, Palestine, Ahlam lives and works in London, and is a renowned champion of peace and human rights. She founded and directs BASIRA – British Arabs Supporting Universal Women's Rights – within which she has stressed the need to combat FGM and curb religious strictures. A former member of the Arab Jewish Forum and Joint Action for Israeli-Palestinian Peace, she has written numerous articles in the Arabic and English press on issues ranging from Israel and Palestine to women's rights in the Middle East.

Ayad Al-Qla'ay - Born in Al Nasyria in southern Iraq in 1987, he is an Arabic language graduate and works as an Arabic teacher. He has published two short story collections and his poetry collection will be published soon.

Safa'a Al Sarai - An icon of the latest Iraqi revolution, Safa'a was killed by gas canister on the 28th of October 2019. Born in 1993, he had secured his first job in computing – his degree subject – a week before his death. His poem was read by a friend from inside a tent named after him in Tahrir Square, Baghdad.

Amer Al-Tayeb was born 1990. He is author of three collections and winner of best poet under the age of 35. He holds a diploma in Accountancy.

Mir Mahfuz Ali - Born in Dhaka, Bangladesh, he is a performance artist, renowned for his extraordinary voice – a rich throaty whisper brought about by a bullet in the throat fired by a Bangladeshi policeman during an anti-war demonstration. He studied in London and at Essex University. He has given readings in London, the Edinburgh Festival, the National Theatre of Slovenia and at other events. His poetry collection is *Midnight, Dhaka* (Seren, 2014). His work has appeared in anthologies and magazines and was shortlisted for the 2007 New Writing Partnership Literature Awards.

Tessy Aura - SocraTess is a vibrational, vivacious and voluptuous poet. Her poetry is a riot, cloaked in humour, rhymes and alliteration but it is all a means to one end, the freedom to be woman and complex. She writes about everything under the sun, except for romance because she feels it's overdone. She believes in alchemy through creativity, so she likes to contribute to spaces in which art is used as a tool for entertainment, connection and transformation. Her other interests include African politics and development, music and dance. @iamsocratess.

Hasan Bamyani - A school teacher in Afghanistan, he was attacked by the Taliban for teaching girls. When he fled in 2001 he was forced to leave his family behind in Iran. In 2006 he finally received leave to remain in Britain. His work has appeared in Exiled Ink magazine and in *The Story of My Life: Refugees Writing in Oxford* (Charlbury, 2005).

Nazand Beghikani is an internationally known poet, having won several poetry prizes, including France's Simone Landrey's Feminine Poetry Prize in 2012. She is an Honorary Senior Research Fellow at Bristol University and also the Vincent Wright Chair and Visiting Professor at Paris's Grande Ecole Sciences Po. Begikhani is a leading researcher on gender-based violence, including honour-based violence in the UK and in Iraq: She has particularly focused on women and war, examining rape and sexual violence during conflict in Iraq and

Syria. She is the principal editor/publisher of a specialised imprint at L'Harmattan: 'Peuples cultures et littératures de l'Orient'.

Anna Blasiak is a poet and translator. She studied Art History in Warsaw, Film Studies in Kraków and Arts Policy and Management in London. She has translated over 40 books from English into Polish and some fiction from Polish into English (as Anna Hyde). She writes poetry in Polish and in English. She helps run European Literature Network and is one of the editors of 'Babiniec Literacki', a Polish website publishing poetry written by women.

Leonardo Boix - Born in Buenos Aires, Argentina, he came to London in 1996 to study. He now reports on British news, politics and culture for the Latin American media. He is published in anthologies, journals and books. He runs poetry workshops for British-Latino school students and has established the collective 'Invisible Presence' for Latino-British poets and writers. He is a founder member of SLAP and performs at many venues and festivals. He was awarded the Keats-Shelley poetry prize in 2019.

Maria Eugenia Bravo-Calderara is a Chilean writer in exile. In 1992 she published her first poetry book in London: *Prayer in the National Stadium*. Her short stories and poems are found in anthologies and periodicals in Chile, Spain, the UK and Europe. Her writing deals with the violence caused by the Chilean dictatorship, exile, love and existential loneliness.

Sofia Buchuck is from Cusco, the Inca capital of Peru. The only Quechua singer in the UK, she also plays Andean and Amazonian instruments. Sofia studied ethnomusicology at the National School of Music, Mexico. She has MAs in Cultural Studies and in Oral History and History Research. She supports human rights and refugee issues. Sofia was the first Hispanic singer to perform at the Royal Opera House. Her educational projects have benefitted the Latin American community. Her oral histories, collected, from refugees, were archived and exhibited at the Museum of London.

Tshaka Campbell - Originally from London, Tshaka is a poet, musician, artist and performer. He has toured internationally and been featured at theatres from the Apollo Theatre, New York to the O2,

London. He has authored several books including *Tarman, Tunnel Vision* and *Letters to my Daughter*. He has recorded three albums entitled *One, Bloodlines* and *Skin vol.1* and collaborated on musical projects in the House, Jazz and Blues genres. He is currently on the Board of Directors for the Poetry Center San Jose and was one of three finalists for the 2020 Santa Clara Poet Laureate. He resides in California.

Kholoud Charaf is a Syrian Druze poet, art critic and activist who fled civil war and chaos in Syria and now has a residency in Germany as part of the PEN Germany programme. She has published four collections including *The Remains of the Butterflies* (2016) and *Return to the Mountains: A Journal in the Shadow of War* (2019) which won the prestigious Ibn Battuta prize and has been translated into five languages. In 2018 she lived in Krakow, Poland as a scholarship holder of ICORN. In 2020 she received the American Artist Protection Foundation.

Handsen Chikowore is from Zimbabwe having fled Zimbabwe through the Limpopo border. He has written poems on topics such as human rights, poverty and animals. He has been published in magazines including *The Spectator, The Parade, The Southern Cross, De La Mancha and Philosophy Now*. Handsen has read his poems at Exiled Writers Ink, Paris Poetry Festival, Limmud, Black History Month and Brecon Poetry Festival.

Ilhan Sami Çomak was arrested in 1994 when he was a student at Istanbul University and charged with starting a forest fire and of being associated with the banned Kurdistan Workers' party, charges he denied and to which he confessed only under torture. Despite evidence of his innocence, and a series of failed or constantly postponed appeals, he is still in prison on the basis of that same confession. He was sentenced to life imprisonment in 2000. Despite his 26 years of prison, Çomak has produced several volumes of highly regarded poetry, the last of them winning the prestigious Sennur Sezer prize in 2019.

Amir Darwish is a poet and writer of Kurdish origin. Born in Aleppo, he came to Britain as an asylum seeker in 2013. Amir holds advanced degrees in history, international relations and creative and life writing.

His poetry collections are *Don't Forget the Couscous* and *Dear Refugee* (Smokestack) and his memoir is *From Aleppo without Love* (2017).

Nour Darwish was born 1991. He holds a degree in Arabic.

Aida Dërguti was born in Kosova in1972 and holds a BA Honours in History from the University of Prishtina. She fled to Switzerland as a refugee while continuing her political activism, joining the Kosovo Liberation Army as a freedom fighter. Helping to build the Self-determination Movement, she rose to leadership positions including first woman Vice President of the Assembly of Kosovo, and she represented the Kosovo Assembly to the Council of Europe. Aida is a member of Kosovo Women's Network. She stepped down from active political life in 2019.

Amna Dumpor was born in 1968 in Mostar, Bosnia and Hercegovina where she was involved in the media and theatre. She worked as a proconsul in Mostar assisting in the evacuation of 10,000 children and vulnerable people during the Bosnian war. She arrived in the UK in 1992, gaining a degree in Contemporary Business and Political Economy and a postgraduate diploma in Refugee Studies. Her first poetry book was *Tears in the Heart* (1998, Mostar). She has been involved in many projects and creative workshops in the UK and abroad and is currently a portal editor.

Stephen Duncan is a poet and sculptor, the son of the poet Beata Duncan, and he has read his poetry widely at festival venues. He studied in London and Rome, has won many prizes in International Poetry Competitions including the Arvon, Bridport and Cardiff, as well as appearing in the Arts Council New Poetry and Pen Anthologies. Published by both Peterloo and Smith/Doorstop he has received an Arts Council Writers Award, is a Hawthornden Fellow and is featured on poetry pf.

Galal El-Behairy is an Egyptian poet and lyricist who was imprisoned in Cairo in March, 2018 and sentenced to three years imprisonment. His charges include blasphemy, spreading false news, and abuse of social media networks all due to his poetry and the lyrics to the song 'Balaha' which is sung by the Egyptian rock singer Ramy Essam. He continues to write poetry from prison.

Aziz Isa Elkun is a poet, writer and academic who is an active member of the exiled Uyghur community in London where he has lived since 2001. Born in East Turkistan (Uyghur Autonomous Region, China), he has published poems, stories, and research articles in Uyghur and English. He is a researcher on the 'Sounding Islam China' project and wrote *Journey from the Danube River to the Orkhun Valley* in Uyghur. He founded The London Uyghur Ensemble and is secretary of International PEN Uyghur Centre and of the Ilham Tohti Institute. He is an affiliate on a British Academy sustainable development project 'Uyghur Meshrep in Kazakhstan'.

Mabel Encinas-Sánchez was born in Mexico and is a migrant poet and writer. She is part of two groups: *Las Juanas* and *SLAP* (Spanish and Latin American Poets and Writers). Mabel works with teachers and families. Her research and teaching are around inclusion of minority communities and education. She has published poetry, short stories, a regular column on current affairs in *The Prisma* online newspaper, and her first children's book, *I am Adila from Gaza* (Victorina Press).

Miriam Frank was born in Barcelona, from a German Jewish mother and a Lithuanian American father, and sought exile in France, Mexico and New Zealand. She graduated in medicine, returned to Europe, married a German artist, and was appointed Senior Lecturer at the Royal London Hospital. Following her retirement, she translated Latin American and Spanish authors and joined Exiled Writers Ink, forming part of its committee for 4-5 years. She is the author of *My Innocent Absence* (Arcadia Books) and *An Unfinished Portrait* (Gibson Square Books), which have appeared in French and Greek editions.

Alex Galbinski is a features writer, sub-editor and copywriter. She previously worked in market research. She writes about social issues, health, food, books, parenting and more.

Yvonne Green is a London born poet whose mother was Egyptian, her father German (raised in France), her maternal grandparents and paternal grandmother formed part of a 2,700 year-old merchant presence in Central Asia; her paternal grandfather was descended from Maimonides. An orthodox Jewess, she grew up in a home where guests of all religions were welcomed by her multilingual family. Her poetry collections are *Jam & Jerusalem* (Smith/Doorstop, 2018), *Honoured* (Smith/Doorstop, 2015) and *The Assay* (Smith/Doorstop, 2010) from which 'Khundal Khon' is reprinted.

Karim Haidari moved to London from Afghanistan living there from the late 1990s until 2007. He has a post-graduate degree in Creative Writing from City University. Karim writes poetry and plays. Two were performed by the National Theatre of Afghanistan; one of them winning him the international playwright award in Tajikistan. An extract was performed at the Bush Theatre in 2012 by Tamasha Theatre group. He has published three books in his native Pashto and his first novel in English is forthcoming. Karim works for the BBC in Afghanistan.

Saleh Abdalahi Hamudi is from the Western Sahara and was educated in Cuba. Frustrated by the stagnant situation and lack of opportunities on his return home from Cuba, he moved to Spain where he now lives in exile. His poetry collection is entitled *La Arena de Tus Huellas* (2009).

Choman Hardi is a Kurdish poet, translator and academic. She has published three volumes of poetry in Kurdish and two in English: *Life for Us* (Bloodaxe 2004) and *Considering the Women* (Bloodaxe 2015). She was shortlisted for the Forward Prize (2016) and has had articles in *Modern Poetry in Translation*. A former chairperson of EWI, she ran creative writing workshops for the British Council in the UK and in Belgium, Czech Republic and India. In 2014 she returned to her home town of Sulaimaniya where she is Chair of the department of English at the American University of Iraq.

Muyesser Abdul'ehed Hendan is a poet, writer and educator. A native of Ghulja in the north of East Turkistan, Hendan completed a medical degree at Beijing University, followed by a Master's at the University of Malaya. After relocating to Turkey in 2013, she resolved to focus on writing and teaching the Uyghur language. Her debut novel, *Kheyr-khosh, quyash* (Farewell, Sun) is the first work of fiction to focus on the internment camps in East Turkistan.

Golrokh Iraee is an Iranian writer and activist who has been arrested
and imprisoned several times. Her husband, Arash Sadeghi. is serving
a 19-year prison sentence for his human rights activism. Arash
Sadeghi suffers a rare form of bone cancer and is very ill. Initially the
couple were held in Evin, able to see each other weekly; in October
2017, Arash Sadeghi was transferred to the even more notorious
Raja'I Shar prison, 50 miles away. Golrokh Iraee was released in April
2019 and rearrested in November 2019. She is currently serving 2.1
years in the notorious Gharchak prison (Veramin).

Maitham Abdul Jabbar was born 1975. He is a journalist and author
of five poetry books. He holds a degree in electrical engineering.

Maria Jastrzębska was born in Warsaw, Poland, and lives in
Brighton. Poet, editor and translator, her collection, *At the Library of
Memories*, (Waterloo Press, 2013) received much critical acclaim. She
also co-edited *Queer in Brighton* (New Writing South 2014) and
translated Justyna Bargielska's *The Great Plan B* (Smokestack 2017).
Her latest collection, *The True Story of Cowboy Hat and Ingénue*, is a
prose poem (Liquorice Fish 2018).

Anba Jawi - Born in Baghdad, she studied Geology at the University
of Baghdad – one of the pioneering women geologists in Iraq. She
worked in the refugee sector for more than 20 years and was honoured
with an MBE on the Queen's birthday list in 2004 for her services.
She writes and publishes in Arabic and English. A chapter from her
novel *The Silver Engraver* was included in the TLC *Free Reads
Anthology* (2019).

Sonja Juric is from Mostar and is a member of the Croatian Writers
Association of Mostar. Her poetry is included in *Let u TROstihu*,
published in Mostar, 2008 and in various web journals.

Ziba Karbassi - Born in Tabriz, Iran, she had to flee in the mid-1980s
and lives in London. She has published seven books of poetry in
Persian and has read her work extensively across Europe and America.
In 2009 she won the Golden Apple poetry prize for Azerbaijan. Her
poems have appeared in many languages and been published in such
journals as *Poetry Review* and *Modern Poetry in Translation*. Her
chapbook *Collage Poems* (2009) was published by Exiled Writers Ink

and a tri-lingual collection *Poesie/Poems* (2011) by Mille Gru. Her work is translated by the poet, Stephen Watts.

Esmail Khoi is a leading Iranian poet in exile. Educated in Iran and England, he began his career as a lecturer in Philosophy. In the 1960s and '70s, as a founding member of the Writers Association of Iran, he opposed the restrictions on intellectual freedom. After the Iranian Revolution however, he found himself living in an even more oppressive political atmosphere. In the early 1980s, he was forced to spend nearly two years in hiding before fleeing in 1983. His anthologies of poetry in English are *Edges of Poetry* (1995), *Outlandia: Songs of Exile* (1999) and *Voice of Exile* (2002).

Berang Kohdamani was a poet who was born in Afghanistan and lived in London from 1995 until his suicide in 2007. He was a lecturer in the Faculty of Literature at the University of Kabul and from 1989 to 1991 was based in Tajikistan working for the Academy of Science on literature matters. His numerous poetry collections include *Greeting to Corn Poppies*, *Spiritual Meaning of Words* and *The Bitter Chapter of God*.

Abdullah Konushevci was born in 1958 and raised in Prishtina, Kosova, studied literature at the University of Zagreb, and worked for many years as a journalist for the Kosova daily newspaper *Rilindja*. He is noted not only as a leading Kosova poet, but also for his essays and writings on Albanian literature and on the Albanian language. Konushevci is author of six volumes of intense verse, the most recent being *Pikat AD* (The Drops AD), Prishtina 2002, with its startling reflections on the 1999 war in Kosova. He has also translated Ernest Hemingway, Rabindranath Tagore and Milovoj Slavicek into Albanian.

Yang Lian, poet and literary critic, grew up in Beijing and struggled through the Cultural Revolution. He began publishing poetry in China in 1979. From 1994, while based in London, he travelled and published widely in English. His major books include *Masks and Crocodile, The Dead in Exile, Where the Sea Stands Still: New Poems, Yi* and *Narrative Poem*. His most recent poems, essays and theoretical writings have been collected and reprinted as *Yang Lian zuopin*. He lives in Berlin.

Valbona Ismaili Luta wrote for the Kosovo students' newspaper *Bota e re* in the 80s. She was a correspondent for Radio France International and writes a column for *Teuta* magazine in Prishtina. She has been a member of the EWI since its beginnings, and a founder of FLO Festival of Literature. She taught Albanian to Foreign Office diplomats deployed to Kosovo/Albania and in colleges. She has a Diploma in Attachment-based Counselling and Postgraduate Studies in Systemic Practice (Family Therapy). Valbona has been working with Wimbledon Guild charity since 2009.

Ahmed Mansoor is an Emirati poet, blogger and human rights activist. In 2017 he was arrested and sentenced to ten years in prison, accused of posting false information on social media which "insulted the status and prestige of the UAE and its symbols." In 2018 his attempt to appeal the sentence failed and he has spent all of his time in solitary confinement since his arrest.

Hilton Mendelsohn was born in 1970 in Bulawayo, Zimbabwe where he wrote for *The Chronicle*. He moved to the UK in 1997 and began work for the Movement for Democratic Change in 2000. He works with various Zimbabwean organisations and is a founder of Writing Wrongs, an exiled Zimbabwean writers' group. He is currently based in Manchester working on an anthology of his poetry.

William Mbwembe came to the UK in 2003 as a refugee from Zimbabwe, where he was a manager in a small company in Harare. He settled in Swansea where he worked in the voluntary sector and helped to establish the African Community Centre, becoming its first manager in 2005. He died in 2007 after a long illness and is buried in Zimbabwe.

Nada Menzalji is a Syrian poet, author, journalist, editor and translator. She left Latakia, her home town, for London in 1998. She is now a freelance journalist at the BBC. She was the poet-guest at the 2019 United Nations' celebration of the International Day of the Arabic Language in Geneva and has taken part in many poetry festivals in Europe and the Middle East. Her published poetry collections in Arabic include *Withered Petals for Dinner* and *Thefts of a Nameless Poet* and her work has appeared in two poetry anthologies in French and an anthology of Syrian poetry from the 1990s.

Kamal Mirawdeli is a British Kurdish poet and writer living in London. He has published four collections of poetry in Kurdish and *Passage to Dawn* in English (2002) as well as books on philosophy, history, literature and politics in Kurdish and English. His father was a nationalist poet and mayor of the town Marga in Iraqi Kurdistan where Kamal was born in 1951. He completed his graduate education as teacher of English at the University of Baghdad. He left Iraq in 1981 and studied literature (MA and PhD) at Essex University and political economy (MSc) at the London School of Economics.

Nkosana Mpofu is a Zimbabwean praise poet who writes in Ndebele/Zulu and English about a broad range of subjects - from rivers, weather, feelings, politics and social issues to faith. He lives in North Shields.

Brikena Muharremi is a Kosovo Albanian who came to the UK as a student when she was 16. She continued her higher education in the UK and qualified as a barrister after she was unable to return to Kosovo due to the war. She is a published poet whose work has been included in a number of publications, including anthologies, in Europe and America. Brikena is the first recipient of the prestigious 'Ambassador of the Nation' Award from the Albanian Government.

O.T. Mukozho (Otilla Tsvegie Slater) was born in 1979 in Zimbabwe. She is a published writer, artist and poet. Author of *Gift of the Past*, she had exhibitions at Matombo and Zimbabwe National Galleries. She left Zimbabwe in 1997 and qualified in Social Work in the UK in 2006 where she now lives.

Biko Mutsaurwa is a leading Shona poet, Hip Hop artist and community activist. He is the founder of UHURU Network, an educational trust that uses cultural activism and popular education to advance the struggle for freedom of expression and social justice in Zimbabwe. He is also one of the initiators of the Afrikan Hiphop Caravan, based upon a strategic orientation towards social movements of the working class and the oppressed.

Elvedin Nezirovic is from Mostar. He has published two collections of poetry and his work appears in literary magazines across the former

Yugoslavia. He worked as a journalist for Radio X, Radio Free
Europe, Radio Studio 88 and *Grace* magazine, Sarajevo.

Nasrin Parvaz, born in Iran, became a civil rights activist who was
subsequently arrested, tortured and spent eight years in prison until
released in 1990 and fled to England in 1993. She obtained a degree in
Psychology and an MA in International Relations. Nasrin's prison
memoir was published in Farsi (2002) and in English (2018) and her
novel *The Secret Letters from X to A* was published in 2019
(Victorina). One of Nasrin's short stories, 'A War against
Womanhood', won the Women's World Award in 2003. Her poems
appeared in *Over Land, Over Sea, Poems for those seeking Refuge*
(2015).

Ghazi Rabihavi was known as a short story writer, novelist and
screenplay writer in Iran. After migrating to the UK, he published
Iranian Four Seasons and *Maryam's Smile* which are banned in Iran.
Harold Pinter produced Rabihavi's play *Look Europe!* which was
internationally performed. *Stoning* is a further play. *Fourplay* (2000)
was performed in London while *Voices* was performed in San
Francisco. *Prey* (2001) is a short film while *Captured by Camera* is
based on the true story of Ahmad Batebi imprisoned for fifteen years
after being photographed at demonstrations. His novel *Boys of Love*
(2019) is banned in Iran.

Born in 1975 in the Western Sahara, **Nanna labat Rachid** has
published three collections of poetry. She studied psychology at the
University of Oran, Algeria and then worked in the Saharawi
Women's Union. In 2007 Nanna became responsible for the literacy
campaign and is currently a director of the Department of Information,
Culture and Orientation.

Shaee Raouf is originally Kurdish Iraqi. She came to the UK at the
age of nine and recently returned to Kurdistan where she is a
registered barrister. She performed her poetry throughout London and
is passionate about Middle Eastern Art and Culture.

Mehrangiz Rassapour, poet, literary critic and editor of *Vajeh*
(Word) magazine, was born in south west Iran. She has published five
collections of poetry. Her works have been translated into many

languages and she has been critically acclaimed. At an international poetry festival in France, she was given the title "The Dawn of Literature" by the newspaper Le Temps (Art and Culture).

Shirin Razavian is a Tehran-born British poet whose work has appeared in *Poetry London, Index on Censorship, Exiled Ink Magazine, The London Magazine, Agenda* and *Persian Book Review* among others. She has published five Farsi and English poetry collections in the UK, the last being *Which Shade of Blue.* Some of her poems have been translated into Czech and published in the anthology *Before Infinity Ends.* Shirin's work has been featured in various anthologies including *Happiness-The Delight Tree, The Poetry of Iranian Women and Silver Throat of the Moon.*

Consuelo Rivera-Fuentes describes herself as an activist, EFL teacher, sociologist, feminist Lesbian, writer and publisher. She has developed a system called *Bibliodiversity* in relation to Victorina Press, the publisher she founded. She loves to 'memory' in company, so supports Las Juanas (feminist literary collective of women), SLAP and Exiled Writers Ink. She teaches English to Syrian refugees in Shropshire and is one of the three Directors of the Festival El Sueño Existe. She is a member of the Autobiography Study Group of the British Sociological Association.

Rafiq Sabir Born in 1950 in Iraqi Kurdistan, he moved to Sweden in 1989. A graduate of Baghdad University, he belongs to the post Abdulla Goran generation of modernists in Kurdish poetry and writes in the Sorani dialect. His poem 'Don't Leave Her Alone' are the lyrics of a popular song. As a member of the Union for Kurdish Writers he organised a festival in Halabja on resistance literature and has published a book on that subject.

Shabibi Shah has a degree in journalism from Kabul University, worked as a teacher in Afghanistan and published her first poems in her native language Dari. She arrived in Britain with her husband and children in 1984 as political refugees. She published her autobiography, *Where do I Belong?* (2001) and her novel, *Innocent Deception* (2014). She established the Help Point for refugees in Croydon and also chaired the Afghan Paiwand Association, dealing with refugees' day to day problems.

Mahvash Sabet Shariari is a Bahai'i community leader and educator who was arrested in 2008 and released in 2017. Her *Prison Poems* were published in 2013, and she is a recipient of the Liu Xiaobo Courage to Write Award, and the PEN Pinter Prize, along with Michael Longley.

Suhrab Sirat - With collections of poems and literary commentaries published in Persian/Dari, Sirat is a writer, journalist and former civil society activist from Afghanistan. He sought asylum in the UK in 2014 and is currently working for the BBC's Persian service. He studied at Balkh University and holds a Masters in International Politics and Human Rights from City, University of London. Suhrab wrote lyrics for the first Afghan female rapper. His first collection of poems in English is being published by Exiled Writers Ink.

Malak Soufi is a poet, journalist, translator, interpreter (Arabic-Spanish) and organiser of cultural activities of the Arab world in Spain. At the 2016 opening of the International Festival of Poetry in Havana, Cuba, she appealed to all present to oppose violence in Syria through the power of poetry. She has produced two anthologies *Mother* and *Salt Boundaries: Poetry by Refugees on Lesbos*. She lives between Turkey and the UK.

Edin Suljic spent his formative years in the multicultural, multinational society of former Yugoslavia, moving to the UK at the onset of the tragic Yugoslavian war in 1991. His creative output includes poetry, short stories and essays; writing for, and producing collaborative theatrical work; as well as photography and short films. His poetry collection, *Personal Things and the Rest*, was published by Hafan Books, 2018. He translated and adapted the diary written by his sister, Elvira Simic, during the war in former Yugoslavia, *Cry of Bosnia* (Genie Quest Publishers, 1998).

Rebecca Taylor is the Editor of *Jewish Renaissance* magazine. She has been a journalist for 25 years, starting at *The Japan Times* in Tokyo. After returning to the UK she worked at *The Guardian* and at *Time Out London*, where she was the News Editor for 10 years. Her work has included interviews with numerous cultural and political figures including Mike Leigh, Naomi Klein, Tony Blair, David Cameron and Boris Johnson.

Alemu Tebeje is an Ethiopian journalist, poet, lyric writer and campaigner and now lives in London. His poems have been published in Amharic, Chinese and English. His first collection is *Greetings to the People of Europe* (Tamrat, 2018). He co-translated and co-edited with Chris Beckett *Songs We learn from Trees: An Anthology of Ethiopian Amharic Poetry* (Carcanet, 2020).

Bogdan Tiganov is a Romanian born British poet and co-founder of Aiurea Press. He has had work published and translated internationally. *Wooden Tongue Speaks* (2008) is a collection of short stories and poetry set in post-Ceausescu and post-Cold War Romania.

Tenzin Tsundue is a Tibetan writer and activist based in Dharamshala, India. The winner of the first Picador-Outlook Non-fiction Contest, he is the author of four books of poetry and stories. Tsundue's writing has been translated into over fifteen languages, anthologised in international literary collections and been prescribed in school and university textbooks. His writing has inspired feature films, plays and novels. He is one of the most jailed writers in India.

Hama Tuma is an Ethiopian poet, satirist, essayist and human rights campaigner living in exile in Paris. He has published three collections of poetry in Amharic and one in English: *Just a Nobody* (2017) is a collection of passionate poems of protest. Tuma has published two highly acclaimed books of short stories including *The Case of the Socialist Witchdoctor* (1993).

Denisse Vargas-Bolaños is a Bolivian poet and writer. She is a member of the feminist literary collective Las Juanas and SLAP (Spanish and Latin American Poets and Writers). She was also part of the Invisible Presence Project. Her poems and short stories have appeared in anthologies, fanzines and magazines such as *Unravelling Memories, Visitantes, A New Voice: Emerging British Latino Writers, Flawa, Latinx Literary Fanzine, Voices* and *Magma*.

Ahmad Masood Wahed - Born in Afghanistan, he studied Politics and International Relations at London Metropolitan University.

Sholeh Wolpé is an Iranian-American poet and playwright. She is the recipient of the 2014 PEN/Heim, 2013 Midwest Book Award and

2010 Lois Roth Persian Translation prize. Her most recent books include *Keeping Time with Blue Hyacinth* (Univ. of Arkansas Press), *The Conference of the Birds* (W.W. Norton) and *Let Me In* (Theaterfolk). Wolpé's literary work numbers over twelve collections of poetry, books of translations, and anthologies, as well as several plays. She is the Writer-in-Residence at University of California at Irvine.

Nahida Yasin was born in Jerusalem and left Palestine as a refugee in 1967 at the age of seven during the Six-Days-War. After living in several different countries, she settled in the UK in 1985 and currently lives in Liverpool. Her poetry collection is entitled *I Believe in Miracles: A Collection of Palestinian Poems*.

Simone Yasmin is a writer, spoken word artist and blogger, born in Leeds. In her blog *Ethereal Truth* she writes about things people leave unsaid, such as racism, feminism and other humanitarian issues. Yasmin uses poetry as escapism and feels content when creating. Her own experiences have helped to shape her work, although more recently she has worked to share the stories of those unable to voice their own.

Nazanin Zaghari-Ratcliffe is an Iranian-British dual citizen who has been detained in Iran since 3 April 2016. In early September 2016 she was sentenced to five years' imprisonment after being found guilty of "plotting to topple the Iranian government." She was temporarily released on 17 March 2020 to house arrest and a trial based on new charges has temporarily been postponed.

Mojawer Ahmad Zyar - Born in Afghanistan in 1937, he graduated from Kabul University in 1959 in linguistics. In 1966 he completed his PhD at the University of Bern, Switzerland, then taught at Humboldt University, Berlin and at the University of Peshawar. Professor Zyar is a prolific writer in Pashto, German and English, an expert in over 100 dialects of Pashto and other Afghan languages, reviving Pashto as a global language and introducing Pashto free style poetry.

Editors

David Clark, child of refugees from Nazi Germany, grew up in England, Italy, and Austria, studied anthropology in Canada and East Africa, edited the Poetry Page for *Second Generation Voices*. His poems are published in *Contemporary Writers of Poland, Flying Between Words*, edited by Danuta Blaszak and Anna Maria Mickiewicz (2015), *Israel Voices* (2019) and in *20th Jubilee Anthology, Contemporary Writers of Poland* (2020).

Catherine Temma Davidson is a novelist and poet who teaches at Regent's University in London and serves as chair of Exiled Writers Ink.

Fatima Hagi is a poet, communications specialist, women's rights activist and mental health advocate who co-founded www.safespacesforblackwomen.com. Fatima was raised in London, but spent her early years in Somalia and Kenya, her ancestral homeland. Her passion for human rights has seen her revisit East Africa, working for the United Nations and using her writing skills to raise awareness of marginalised societies. In 2019, Fatima managed the Somali Week Festival, an annual arts festival run in London as part of Black History Month.

Dr Jennifer Langer is founding director of Exiled Writers Ink and editor of four anthologies of exiled literature. She holds a doctorate in Cultural Memory from SOAS, University of London, and is a SOAS Research Associate. Her published poetry collection, *The Search*, is forthcoming.

Esther B Lipton - Her poetry and short stories are published in national and international anthologies. She co-edited Exiled Writers magazine and is a reviewer and editor and currently leads a Creative Writing group for the University of the Third Age.

Danielle Maisano is a U.S. born novelist, poet and journalist currently residing in London. She is a former member of the U.S. Peace Corps (2011-2013 Togo) and holds an MA in International Relations from the School of Oriental and African Studies. Her work has appeared in *Exiled Ink* E-magazine and *Shado* magazine. Her debut novel, *The*

Ardent Witness, was published by Victorina Press and was a finalist for the 2019 International Book Awards fiction category.

Dr Denise Saul is a writer and poet. Her *White Narcissi* (Flipped Eye) was Poetry Book Society Pamphlet Choice and *House of Blue* (Rack Press) was PBS Pamphlet Recommendation. She is a Geoffrey Dearmer Prize winner. Denise holds a doctorate in creative writing (poetry) from University of Roehampton.

Palewell Press

Palewell Press is an independent publisher handling poetry, fiction and non-fiction with a focus on books that foster Justice, Equality and Sustainability. The Editor can be reached on enquiries@palewellpress.co.uk